Making A
Just Peace

Human & Rights
Domination
Systems

Bought on
10/31/98

Making A Just Peace

Human & Rights Domination Systems

C. Dale White

Abingdon Press
Nashville

Making a Just Peace: Human Rights and Domination Systems

This book is printed on recycled, acid-free paper.

0-687-03133-8

Scripture quotations are from the New Revised Standard Version Bible. Copyright 1989 by the Division of Christian Education of the National Council of the Churches of Christ in the USA. Used by permission.

This study is dedicated to esteemed colleages and dear friends of the general boards and agencies of The United Methodist Church, including the Council of Bishops, who faithfully lead the denomination in ministries of justice, peace, and the integrity of creation. Special gratitude is offered to the directors, staff, and officers of the Women's Division of the General Board of Global Ministries. They lead one of the largest women's organizations in the United States, noted for its commitment to global justice and human rights.

99 00 01 02 03 04 05 06 07 — 10 9 8 7 6 5 4 3 2 1

MANUFACTURED IN THE UNITED STATES OF AMERICA

Foreword

But when Jesus saw this, he was indignant and said to them, "Let the little children come to me; do not stop them; for it is to such as these that the kingdom of God belongs. Truly I tell you, whoever does not receive the kingdom of God as a little child will never enter." And he took them up in his arms, laid his hands on them, and blessed them. (Mark 10:14-16)

Then they came to Jerusalem. And he entered the temple and began to drive out those who were selling and those who were buying in the temple, and he overturned the tables of the money changers and the seats of those who sold doves; and he would not allow anyone to carry anything through the temple. He was teaching and saying, "Is it not written,
    'My house shall be called a house
        of prayer for all the nations'?
    But you have made it a den of robbers."
(Mark 11:15-17)

The image of a laughing Jesus with children in his arms is part of our earliest memories and remains to this day the most comforting one. This image is in sharp contrast to those in newspapers and televisions today—of children shooting children and of millions of children suffering the world over—much of it caused by people of faith, some of whom follow Jesus.

Dr. Mahbub ul Hap, former Special Adviser to the United Nations Development Programme, reminds us in his "Reflections on Human Development":
◆ We live in a world where so many children are denied their very childhood, yet societies often choose to spend much more on arms than on the education and health of their children.
◆ We live in a world where nations can easily find the financial resources for air-conditioned jeeps for their military generals, yet fail to find the resources for even windowless schoolrooms for their children.
◆ We live in a world where, when children cry for milk in the middle of the night, their military generals are out shopping for tanks.
    The focus of this book by Bishop C. Dale White is not only on the quality of life

for peoples today, but also on "the rights of future generations [the children] to inherit a world in which both liberty and the abundant life are assured." Dale urges his readers to put faces on the poor children. And the "faces" he recalls are of barefoot children playing alongside open sewers in India; of children in refugee camps in Zimbabwe and Sierra Leone; of homeless boys in the streets of Rio de Janeiro; of children in crowded classrooms in Bangladesh.

But the author does not forget the faces of poor children in the United States. At the end of the chapter on poverty, Dale asks, "Is poverty a problem in the so-called Third World countries only?" He raises many such questions at the end of each chapter and in the study guides for those wishing to reflect and act on ways to make a just peace in our world.

This is also a book of stories—many of them autobiographical. Each chapter begins with a story about an experience that made an impact on the life of Bishop Dale While. And so—as we write this foreword—we, too, feel impelled to tell stories that are meaningful to us and remind us of the contrasting images of Jesus Christ that we think are reflected in this wonderful book.

Our first story is a folk tale. Jesus himself used such stories to impart his message, and people the world over use folk tales to make their points. In all cultures, there is a character about whom stories are told. He is usually known as the "village fool"—and makes people laugh—but there is always some moral twist to the story that makes the character into a hero.

One such folk-character is well known throughout North Africa. He is called by different names in different countries, but he behaves the same way in all of them. In Algeria, his name is Djeha. One day, Djeha needed to raise money for a young girl who had become an orphan. He went to each house in the village, asking for money to help this young girl. He finally came to the house of the rich man in the village. The rich man kicked Djeha out the door, shouting, "That's for you!" Djeha picked himself up, turned to the rich man, and said, "Okay, that's for me. But what will you give the orphan girl?"

Today, all over the world, doors are being slammed shut in the faces of children by the selfishness, greed, and cruelty of adults—and no one comes to open them. No one apologizes, no one holds them, and no one wipes their tears. Children shoot children; children go to war; children work in garbage dumps; children starve; children are homeless; children have no clothes; and children have no one to care for them. Violations of the human rights of children are the greatest crimes of humankind and a denial of the fullness of life for generations to come.

This is why Dale's book is significant: because it is written for and about people who are caring—and who have hope. And hope is like a door that can be opened from both sides. We can open it ourselves and walk across the threshold—or it may be opened by caring persons—and together we walk across the threshold. The important thing is that people of hope do not give up before a closed door; they refuse to accept the world as it is. People of hope are a "struggling" people. They are people who believe in the reign of God in their time. They, like the laughing Jesus, take the children in their arms and move forward.

A contrasting image that comes to mind is that of an angry Christ. This image was popularized on the island of Negros in the Philippines, through a painting by an artist among the *sakadas*, the sugar plantation workers whose livelihoods were threatened on an ongoing basis by fluctuating world market prices and the anti-farmer laws of the Marcos government. These were workers whose family needs could not be met by wages that were less than meager, declining almost to starvation levels. These farm workers were caught in this desperate situation, when the price of sugar in the world market dipped so low in the 1970s and the 1980s that many landlords shifted to products multinational corporations deemed exportable (e.g., prawns), leaving the sugar workers jobless. In this real-life story, world trade prices dictate life and death to the Filipino sugar workers. and they were forced to borrow money at rates so exorbitant that it mired generations of *sakada* families in a constant cycle of escalating debt.

The *sakadas* identified with the angry Christ of the Gospel, who "overturned the tables of the money changers" who had made God's Temple into a "den of robbers"; they found in the angry Christ one who was in solidarity with them in their resolve. It is this same angry resolve that many peoples and civil society organizations maintain around the world—the ongoing resolve they all have to promote human rights and uphold human dignity, to eradicate poverty, to overcome militarism, to address the environmental crisis, to challenge patriarchy—and rid the world of domination systems. This is what Dale White's book is all about.

The depth and breadth of the issues and concerns addressed in *Making a Just Peace* make it compelling reading for anyone concerned about the future of the earth—and who hopes that we may bequeath to the children of the world a better future than our past. Dale insists that "the aim is to protect the global commons—the common heritage of the entire human family." By indicting the systems of domination that create war and poverty, that destroy our environment and perpetuate racism and sexism, Dale offers human rights as standards to work toward in achieving a just peace:

◆ The people of the world have a right to equitable and sustainable economic and social development!
◆ The people of the world have a right to peace!
◆ The people of the world have the right to a healthy and productive life in harmony with nature!

This is a very special publication for United Methodists, too, because in this year of the celebration of the fiftieth anniversary of the *Universal Declaration of Human*

Foreword

Rights, Dale White's book provides them with an opportunity to reflect on some of the "life" of the church, through the eyes and heart of one of its activist bishops (also known as the farmer from Iowa who created the "In Defense of Creation" garden at the Women's Division Scarritt-Bennett Center in Nashville, Tennessee). Twelve years have passed since Dale, acting with the Council of Bishops of The United Methodist Church, presented the challenging statement and study entitled *In Defense of Creation: The Nuclear Crisis and a Just Peace.* And six years have now passed since the Council issued its 1992 Episcopal Address on "Domination Systems: the demonic systems controlling the world." To this, add a belated indictment of patriarchy. Then put all of these together, and you will have Bishop White's poignant contribution to a better future: *Making a Just Peace: Human Rights and Domination Systems.*

The images of a laughing Jesus and an angry Christ are powerful icons that define for us the gift that Bishop Dale White shares in his book. Anger reminds us of the cost of discipleship—the price that one pays in naming and confronting demonic systems of domination in our world. And laughter celebrates the incredible possibility that people of faith will have the hope and strength to work together in "making a just peace."

Mia Adjali and Liberato Bautista
United Methodist Office for the United Nations
March 1998

Contents

Chapter 1

Making a Just Peace: Seeking Human Rights

All human beings are born free and equal in dignity and rights.
—The Universal Declaration of Human Rights

Peacemaking is a sacred calling of the gospel . . . making us evangelists of *shalom*.
—In Defense of Creation

More than 110 United Methodists had gathered in front of the South African Consulate in New York City. The long and difficult struggle against the apartheid system in South Africa was gaining momentum in the United States. Hundreds of groups were demonstrating; many were engaging in civil disobedience. We were the largest group to demonstrate at the consulate to date. The day was cold and snowy, but that did not prevent a large number of older persons from joining us. We sang hymns as we blocked the entrance to the building. The police were sympathetic. From time to time the police captain would ask, "Is it time now, Reverend?" We would say, "No, we want to sing a few more hymns."

Finally we were ready, and the police captain read us our rights and bundled us into the waiting paddy wagons. I remember the radiance on the faces of the elderly participants as they crowded into the police vans. At last they could act on their convictions! Later, at the station where we were booked, as the last ones filed out of the building an officer was overheard to say, "Wasn't that a sweet group?" Another said, "Yes, and they sang well, too." When we arrived in the courthouse some weeks later to answer our summons, the judge threw out our indictment and gave a stern lecture against the apartheid system. A layperson in one of the congregations of the New York Conference was upset when he learned that his pastor had been arrested. He said, "I was going to complain to the District Superintendent, but I found out he was arrested, too. Then I was going to complain to the bishop, but even he was arrested."

Later, in June 1994, I was invited to the White House Conference on Africa. There I heard Salim Ahmed Salim, Secretary General of the Organization of African Unity, speak. He paid a warm tribute to the people of the United States, including the churches, for the vigorous campaign they had waged against the apartheid government of South Africa. Congressional action to force economic sanctions on that government played a key role in bringing down a vicious system of legalized racism. A reluctant Congress would not have taken that action apart from the campaign coordinated by the TransAfrica coalition, which mobilized thousands of American citizens to insist on a change. The people had spoken. Nelson Mandela, courageous leader of the freedom struggle in his country and now president of the Republic of South Africa, sent a message to the White House Conference:

> In as much as we were partners in the struggle against apartheid and in as much as we were inspired by the ideals of the U.S. founding fathers, we believe that a new and more challenging partnership is emerging between our two nations on issues of human rights and economic development. . . . In a sense, human rights, including socioeconomic issues, have become the focal point of international relations. They are, after all, the guarantee to domestic, regional, and international peace and stability.

Struggles to achieve human rights are the central focus of this study. Three convictions guide us: (1) Human rights are the guarantor for a just peace and sustainable development. (2) Demonic systems hold the human family captive, robbing them of their dignity, freedom, and prosperity. (3) Courageous, vigorous, organized citizen action can break the backs of those systems, in the United States and around the world.

STRUGGLING FOR HUMAN RIGHTS

Fifty-three years ago the world was staggering to recover from the ravages of the Second World War. Much of Europe lay in ruins. Most of the major cities of Japan had perished in the flames of incendiary bombs. Then Hiroshima and Nagasaki were incinerated in the first hostile use of nuclear weapons. The human capacity to destroy had grown beyond the power of the imagination to comprehend it, much less to control it.

The nations of the world gathered in San Francisco to create a new instrument for global cooperation, declaring in the Preamble to the Charter of the United Nations:

We, the peoples of the United Nations determined

to save succeeding generations from the scourge of war, which twice in our lifetime has brought untold sorrow to mankind, and
to reaffirm faith in fundamental human rights, in the dignity and worth of the human person, in the equal rights of men and women and of nations large and small, and
to establish conditions under which justice and respect for the obligations arising from treaties and other sources of international law can be maintained, and
to promote social progress and better standards of life in larger freedom,

And for these ends,

to practice tolerance and live together in peace with one another as good neighbors, and
to unite our strength to maintain international peace and security, and
to ensure, by the acceptance of principles and the institution of methods, that armed force shall not be used, save in the common interest, and

to employ international machinery for the promotion of the economic and social advancement of all peoples,
Have resolved to combine our efforts to accomplish these aims.

Three years later, on December 20, 1948, the vow to "reaffirm faith in fundamental human rights" came to fruition as the UN General Assembly adopted the *Universal Declaration of Human Rights.* Now, to commemorate the fiftieth anniversary of that historic moment, you are invited to reflect upon the impact of the first global commitment to universal human rights.

The first statements in the Preamble to the *Declaration* establish the grounding for the thirty Articles that follow:

Whereas recognition of the inherent dignity and of the equal and inalienable rights of all members of the human family is the foundation of freedom, justice and peace in the world,
Whereas disregard and contempt for human rights have resulted in barbarous acts which have outraged the conscience of mankind, and the advent of a world in which human beings shall enjoy freedom of speech and belief and freedom from fear and want has been proclaimed as the highest aspiration of the common people.

Articles 1 and 2 restate this principle:

Article 1.
All human beings are born free and equal in dignity and rights. They are endowed with reason and conscience and should act towards one another in a spirit of brotherhood.
Article 2.
Everyone is entitled to all the rights and freedoms set forth in this Declaration, without distinction of any kind, such as race, colour, sex, language, religion, political or other opinion, national or social origin, property, birth or other status.

The universality of human rights is clearly expressed. "Human rights," unlike other "rights," which can be earned, purchased, or granted by others, come with birth. Every person without exception is entitled to them by virtue of being human.

The language is familiar now. During the Iran hostage crisis, we saw these words

> *"Human rights are the rights and freedoms that allow us to fully develop and use our human qualities, our intelligence, our talents, and our conscience and to satisfy our spiritual and other needs. They belong to everyone and are the equal and inalienable rights of all members of the human family."*
>
> —United Nations definition.

printed on banners along the walls of the American embassy in Teheran. It was Christmas 1979, and seven of us were bringing a message of peace to the Ayatollah Khomeini. Walking along the sidewalk beside the embassy, we passed booth after booth, each show-casing a freedom movement somewhere on earth—Africa, Latin America, Asia, and North America. The words claimed most often by these movements for liberation came from Thomas Jefferson, who in setting out the reasons for the American Revolution, wrote in the Declaration of Independence:

We hold these truths to be self-evident, that all men are created equal, that they are endowed by their Creator with certain unalienable Rights, that among these are Life, Liberty, and the Pursuit of Happiness.

As I walked from booth to booth in Teheran, I reflected on the inspiration these words have brought to movements for liberation across the years. Later, I strolled among the markers in the Beheshti Zahra cemetery, honoring the 50,000 young men and women who had died in the Iranian revolution. I pondered the long years of struggle and pain courageous people have suffered in achieving each hard-won gain for human rights. Elites who wield exploitative power never willingly surrender it. The road to human dignity is lined with persons of uncommon vision and incredible courage. At great personal risk, they challenged demonic systems of discrimination and oppression. Think of these milestones in the evolution of human rights:

◆ the Magna Charta
◆ the peasant rebellions under Jan Hus in Central Europe in the 15th century
◆ the Protestant Reformation of the 16th century
◆ the bourgeoisie revolutions of the 18th century
◆ The French declaration of the rights of man and of the citizen (1789)
◆ The American Declaration of Independence and the Constitution
◆ the Abolitionist movement for the liberation of the slaves in the late 19th century
◆ the labor movement of the 19th century
◆ the Suffragette movement in the early 20th century

♦ the brutal struggle to liberate the victims of Fascist, Nazi, and Japanese aggression in World War II
♦ the wars of liberation from colonial rulers in Africa, Asia, and Latin America
♦ the civil rights movement in the U.S. in the 1960s
♦ the feminist movement in the 1970s and 1980s and the ongoing struggle for women's rights around the globe
♦ the achievements for human rights in Eastern Europe and the former Soviet Union in the 1980s and early 1990s
♦ the struggle to overcome the apartheid system in South Africa
♦ the recent liberation struggles in Central America, sub-Saharan Africa, and Myanmar
♦ the continuous struggle for the rights of racial/ethnic and indigenous peoples all over the world

Reflecting upon those who in every age spoke truth to power and with great courage stood up for human rights, I thought of Hebrews 11. Here we read a litany of praise for those who walked by faith, guided by "the assurance of things hoped for, the conviction of things not seen." "Time would fail me," the apostle wrote, to mention all those who "through faith conquered kingdoms, administered justice, obtained promises, shut the mouths of lions, quenched raging fire, escaped the edge of the sword, won strength out of weakness, became mighty in war, put foreign armies to flight" (Heb. 11:33).

The Role of the Churches

We in the Christian community should not be surprised if the words in the Preamble to the *Universal Declaration* sound familiar. The words express ideals that are deeply rooted in our faith, ideals of "the inherent dignity and of the equal and inalienable rights of all members of the human family." This is "the foundation of freedom, justice and peace in the world."

These convictions are central to the Judeo-Christian faith. It is no accident that they appear in the UN document. Devoted church leaders worked tirelessly to see that they were included. Several ecumenical church agencies played a part as well.

In 1944, the Federal Council of Churches, predecessor to the National Council of the Churches of Christ in the United States (NCCC), created the Commission to Study the Bases of a Just and Durable Peace, chaired by John Foster Dulles. Fourteen Methodists participated in the commission, including its executive secretary, Walter W. VanKirk. Among the group were people who are well-known to this day: Bishop G. Bromley Oxnam, Ernest F. Tittle, Georgia Harkness, Albert E. Day, and John R. Mott. This commission issued in 1943 a document that included a set of principles, the "Six Pillars of Peace." These principles were studied in congregations, in church councils, and by political leaders of the time. Among the principles was a call for a United Nations structure to assure the peace of nations. In addition, the document advocated a global agreement to bring into harmony economic policies of national governments that have an impact on the international community. The "Six Pillars" included a reformation of global treaties, autonomy for subject peoples, and the control of military establishments everywhere. Finally, the commission declared: "The peace must establish in principle, and seek to achieve in practice, the right of individuals everywhere to religious and intellectual liberty."

The "Six Pillars of Peace" was made a part of the discussions at Dumbarton Oaks in Washington, D.C., in 1944, which laid the foundation for the United Nations Charter. The following year, the Commission on a Just and Durable Peace convened a national study conference. The resulting "Message to the Churches," defining Christian values and advocating principles to be included in the UN Charter, spoke of the purposes of justice and human welfare; progress of colonial and dependent peoples toward autonomy, human rights, and fundamental freedoms; universal membership in the United Nations; reduction of armaments; and protection of small nations.

As preparations were made for the San Francisco Conference, where the UN would be launched, agreement was reached to allow 42 national organizations to send delegates. The Federal Council of Churches was included, and a number of prominent Methodists were included. According to the Rev. Dwain Epps of the World Council of Churches:

> *The vision of a peaceful world where lion and lamb lie down together led to the founding of the United Nations fifty years ago. The vision remains to this day despite wars and removal of walls. For the churches, the United Nations with all of its fragility has been over the years that place where nation states sought peace and cooperation. Churches have contributed to the UN and have worked and prayed that the UN might live up to its high calling. . . . Churches were present at the beginning, contributing to the language of the UN Charter. We maintained steadfast support for international cooperation during the difficult years of the Cold War.*
>
> —Joan Brown Campbell, General Secretary, NCCC

Through collaboration with other non-governmental consultants, the church representatives were successful in having virtually all of their recommendations incorporated into the Charter. A preamble was added along the recommended lines, and more than one observer credited the international Christian influence with having played a determining part in achieving the more extensive provisions for human rights and fundamental freedoms that ultimately found their way into the charter.[1]

The Charter of the UN provides a permanent system for consultation with non-governmental organizations. With that in mind, the World Council of Churches asked for a joint commission to be formed to help to shape the stance of the churches on international affairs. It would participate "in the continuing ministry of Christ in the world of priestly intercession, prophetic judgment, the arousing of hope and conscience and pastoral care for mankind." This Commission of the Churches on International Affairs (CCIA), along with Eleanor Roosevelt and others, set out to press for the adoption of the *Universal Declaration of Human Rights.* Church leaders played a key role in drafting the *Declaration* and providing the article on religious liberty.

As we sit in the pews or preach from the pulpits of local congregations, it is easy to believe that we can have no role in shaping international affairs. Reviewing church influence in shaping the *Universal Declaration of Human Rights* should encourage us to believe that our witness can be heard, however. Our support and encouragement of denominational and ecumenical leaders who serve us near centers of power is the key. We are justified in expecting that they will provide theological reflection, information, and guidance to enable us to shape our own convictions. They will be ambassadors for our Christian conscience as they speak truth to power. Ministering for almost three decades at the General Church level has left me with a profound sense of admiration for colleagues who have accepted this assignment.

The delegates to the General Conference of The United Methodist Church establish the policies that guide leaders in their witness. Those delegates shaped the Social Principles of the denomination. Acknowledging the vital function of government for ordering society, the General Conference, through the Social Principles, declared its commitment to human rights:

Basic Freedoms—We hold governments responsible for the protection of the rights of the people to free and fair elections and to the freedoms of speech, religion, assembly, communications media, and petition for redress of grievances without fear of reprisal; to the right to privacy; and to the guarantee of the rights to adequate food, clothing, shelter, education, and health care. The form and the leaders of all governments should be determined by exercise of the right to vote guaranteed to all adult citizens. We also strongly reject domestic surveillance and intimidation of political opponents by governments in power and all other misuses of elective or appointive offices. The use of detention and imprisonment for the harassment and elimination of political opponents or other dissidents violates fundamental human rights. Furthermore, the mistreatment or torture of persons by governments for any purpose violates Christian teaching and must be condemned and/or opposed by Christians and churches wherever and whenever it occurs.

17

The Church regards the institution of slavery as an infamous evil. All forms of enslavement are totally prohibited and shall in no way be tolerated by the Church.[2]

In the Social Principles, The United Methodist Church declares its commitment to "work toward societies in which each person's value is recognized, maintained, and strengthened." The basic rights of all persons to adequate housing, education, employment, medical care, legal redress for grievances, and physical protection are affirmed. Those singled out for special concern include racial and ethnic minorities, religious minorities, children, youth, young adults, the aging, women, persons with handicapping conditions, and homosexual persons.

A Theological Mandate

In the ecumenical church, one of the most succinct theological statements encouraging our witness for human rights is that of the National Council of the Churches of Christ in the United States (NCCC). In its policy statement, *Human Rights: The Fulfillment of Life in the Social Order*, the NCCC declares:

> Christians believe that human beings are made in the image of God, that every person is of intrinsic worth before God, and that every individual has a right to the fullest possible opportunities for the development of life abundant and eternal. Denial of rights and freedoms that inhere in an individual's worth before God are not simply a crime against humanity; they are a sin against God.

The NCCC goes on to insist that anything that "violates life, denying or limiting its fulfillment, violates God's intention for life." The *Universal Declaration of Human Rights* affirms that "the recognition of the inherent dignity and of the equal and inalienable rights of all members of the human family is the foundation of freedom, justice and peace in the world." The NCCC reminds us that these are recurrent biblical themes, running like a litany throughout Scripture. The biblical mandate to witness and to struggle for human rights rests on these biblical teachings:

- ◆ The creation narratives remind us that we are created in the image and likeness of God, and hence we are equal in God's sight and in God's care.
- ◆ The gift of freedom enables us to choose between good and evil, right and wrong, and thus makes us responsible for our actions.
- ◆ The Sinai narratives establish a covenant people with a sacred calling to care for those in need, especially the widowed, the orphaned, the sick, the poor, the powerless, the sojourner.
- ◆ The Ten Commandments establish the limits of human responsibility and the standards of social life.
- ◆ The prophets call us to do justice, to love mercy, and to walk humbly before God.

◆ In the incarnation, God sent Jesus Christ into the world to show us the way to abundant life. His ministry of service, healing, helping, liberation, and forgiveness is our model.

◆ By the inspiration of his sacrificial love on the cross, the power of the resurrection, and the presence of the Holy Spirit, Jesus enables us to love as God loves. We are empowered to fulfill our calling "to be faithful stewards, selfless servants, obedient peacemakers and articulate advocates."

The Focus of This Study

The primary focus of this study is the human rights, including the rights of future generations. This speaks of the rights of future generations to inherit a world in which both liberty and abundant life are assured. The aim is to protect the global commons—the common heritage of the entire human family. In a world of war, people long for peace and disarmament. In a world where the majority of people live in abject poverty, we long for a just and sustainable economic order. In a world where unrestrained consumerism, careless industrial production, and militarism squander natural resources and despoil the earth, people long for environmental restoration. We will study the massive interlocking systems that threaten the future of the human family in all three areas.

The increasing concentration of wealth in a small segment of the world's population leaves millions destitute. The global economy is a case study in injustice. It guarantees that more than a billion people struggle to survive in abject poverty. Any disturbance of the order, such as drought or civil strife, pushes them over the edge, even to the point of massive starvation. *The people of the world have a right to equitable and sustainable economic and social development!*

The brutality of this century and the militarization of the world, culminating in the threat of nuclear war, have given the quest for peace a new urgency. The absurdity of nation-states seeking to protect their "national security" while threatening to destroy human civilization and endangering the biosphere has become obvious. This has prompted urgent action for disarmament, peacemaking, and peacekeeping. Nations are increasingly being asked to surrender voluntarily a modicum of national sovereignty in the interest of global survival. *The people of the world have a right to peace!*

The uncontrolled development of commerce and industry is destroying the world's eco-systems. Runaway consumerism is using up nonrenewable natural resources at an accelerating pace. The industrial system that sustains this consumerism is laying waste vast areas of fertile land and depriving millions of persons air fit to breathe and water fit to drink. *The people of the world have the right to a healthy and productive life in harmony with nature!*

MAKING A JUST PEACE

Think back to 1986, back over a little more than a decade, an amazing decade in human history. The Council of Bishops of The United Methodist Church was moved to engage in an extraordinary intervention in the life of the Church and the wider society. A small article on the back pages of the *New York Times* spoke of a gathering in Washington, D.C., of over a hundred scientists. They cried alarm at computer models that revealed that a major nuclear interchange could destroy much of life on planet earth. The term *nuclear winter* entered our vocabulary.

Scientists warned that a nuclear war could release millions of tons of smoke into the atmosphere, cutting off sunlight and starving plants, animals, and people. The earth could suffer a second great dying time, rivaling the catastrophe that destroyed the dinosaurs. To amass such destructive power and to threaten its use seemed to us the essence of blasphemy. It is a wanton challenge to the Creator God, who breathed life into being and who yearns for *shalom* on earth. After two years of intensive study and prayer, the bishops sent a pastoral letter to the churches, entitled *In Defense of Creation*:

> "We write in defense of creation. We do so because the creation itself is under attack. Air and water, trees and fruits and flowers, birds and fish and cattle, all children and youth, women and men live under the darkening shadows of a threatening nuclear winter."[3]

The bishops called upon Christian people to become evangelists of *shalom*, the biblical revelation that the Creator God is present in power to bring positive peace, a joyful peace, a just peace to the whole creation. We reminded the people that we are followers of Jesus Christ, the Prince of Peace, who commands us to love our enemies and who promises the richest blessings to peacemakers.

The video released along with the study document was also entitled *In Defense of Creation*. It opens with a United Methodist woman, Doris Akers, standing beside railroad tracks in a small Texas town. She is keeping an all-night prayer vigil, waiting for the nuclear train. Not many miles from her family's ranch near Follette, Texas, was the Pantex Plant in Amarillo. In that place, all of the nuclear warheads piling up in our arsenals were being assembled. The parts came in on a night train, at first called the White Train. For months, prayer vigils were held all over the country, waiting beside the tracks for the trains that all prayed would never come again.

Doris and her rancher husband, Robert, were faithful witnesses for peace, encouraging the organizers of the Peace Farm, which kept vigil across the road from the Pantex Plant. They were also dedicated environmentalists; Robert was the county officer advocating for the protection of ranch land. They understood well the threat to the biosphere posed by nuclear weapons. As the video opens, the dawn is awakening. The nuclear train roars past her. Doris says: "There's something about being there as an act of faith, as making a witness. It's something I can do. I would hate to think that I knew about the possible annihilation of our entire world, with my family, of everything we know and love, and I didn't do one thing to stop it!"

We had no illusions about the potential impact of our peace pastoral. Movements for social change seldom come from leaders of organizations, but from the grass-roots. Yet we could play a validating role. From a group of church leaders, usually seen to represent a mainstream, conservative perspective, we could encourage the millions of grassroots activists like Doris and Robert. The hundreds of letters of gratitude that flooded into our offices from peace coalitions across the country and from around the world convinced us that we were right. It was important for us to say, "We care! We are with you in your struggle." With Doris Akers, we would say, "It was something we could do."

Our study received an overwhelming response. More than 90 percent of our congregations read or printed the pastoral letter; many formed study groups to discuss the issues raised in the Foundation Document. The world press engaged in weeks of debate. The study was translated into six languages and was discussed even in the Soviet Union and Eastern Europe. A series of dialogues ensued with the nuclear community in Oak Ridge. It appeared that the country was overcoming its nuclear numbness and coming awake to the intolerable state of insecurity we had created in the name of national security.

In the nuclear study, the bishops were encouraged by the long history of opposition to war of the United Methodist people, reaching back to John Wesley himself. While The United Methodist Church has not consistently maintained a traditional pacifist position, in its Social Principles we read:

We believe war is incompatible with the teachings and example of Christ. We therefore reject war as an instrument of national foreign policy and insist that the first moral duty of all nations is to resolve by peaceful means every dispute that arises between or among them; that human values must outweigh military claims as governments determine their priorities; that the militarization of society must be challenged and stopped; that the manufacture, sale, and deployment of armaments must be reduced and controlled; and that the production, possession, or use of nuclear weapons be condemned.[4]

The bishops engaged in two years of intensive study and prayer in the preparation of *In Defense of Creation*. As a part of that effort, we held a hearing in Washington, D.C., in which twenty-five expert witnesses testified and background papers from over one hundred consultants were received. In all that time, we heard no one openly advocate the actual use of nuclear weapons. As a former SAC bomber pilot said to us, "Even as we flew through the night, we knew we must never use those horrible weapons. Yet we had no other way to deter the Soviets from using theirs or blackmailing us with the threat to do so."

The *doctrine of deterrence* was the only rationalization for stockpiling nuclear weapons and maintaining a vast network of delivery systems. The terribly expensive and dangerous nuclear superstructure the United States government deployed had only one announced purpose: to convince the Soviets that we had the capability and will, if necessary, to retaliate if attacked.

The Roman Catholic bishops, in their 1983 pastoral *The Challenge of Peace: God's Promise and Our Response*, had developed an interim ethic justifying deterrence. They had written: "In current conditions, 'deterrence' based on balance, certainly not as an end in itself but as a step on the way toward a progressive disarmament, may still be judged morally acceptable." While the Roman Catholic bishops insisted that their position was "a strictly conditioned moral acceptance of nuclear deterrence," hawkish elements within the government immediately claimed the moral authority of the church to justify current policies.

We could not bring ourselves to accept the morality of the deterrence doctrine under any circumstances. We insisted: "The ideology of deterrence must not receive the churches' blessing, even as a temporary warrant for holding on to nuclear weapons."[5] We reasoned that

> *Nuclear deterrence* has too long been reverenced as the idol of national security. . . . [It] has blinded its opponents to the many-sided requirements of genuine security. There can be no unilateral security in the nuclear age. Security requires economic strength and stability, environmental and public health, educational quality, social well-being, public confidence, and global cooperation.[6]

Peace Requires Justice

From the beginning of the study, the Council of Bishops heard from many church leaders in the developing world, including some of our own members. They said that our witness for peace would lose credibility if it did not address the effect of the arms race on the poor of the world. In fact, some spoke disparagingly of the Western preoccupation with a nuclear holocaust that might strike the industrial nations in the future. They accused us of ignoring the scourge of human suffering and death, already decimating huge populations in the poor nations.

We noted a strong tendency for polarization in the United States between those working for peace and those working for justice. We remembered the vicious criticism leveled at Martin Luther King, Jr., when he added the campaign against the war in Vietnam to his demands for social justice for the poor and for African Americans and other minorities. We vowed to show that the nuclear arms race and the larger militarization of the world are a great source of injustice. To quote *In Defense of Creation*, reorganized here for emphasis:

> *The nuclear arms race is an issue of social justice.*
> Justice is *offended* in the double standard under which some nations presume nuclear weapons for themselves while denying them to others.
> Justice is *outraged* in the unending vertical proliferation of nuclear weapons by the superpowers in violation of Article VI of the Non-Proliferation Treaty.
> Justice is abused in the overwhelming power of nuclear-weapon states to threaten the self-determination, security, and very life of nonaligned and nonbelligerent nations.
> Justice is *forsaken* in the squandering of wealth in the arms race while a holocaust of hunger, malnutrition, disease, and violent death is destroying the world's poorest peoples.
> Justice is *defiled* by the superpowers' implication in conventional arms races and proxy wars in the Third World, causing much present suffering and threatening escalation into a nuclear war.[7]

Guiding Principles for a Just Peace

The Council of Bishops of The United Methodist Church went on to discuss the principles for a just peace. Through months of searching the Scriptures and examining our historical traditions, we developed a list of principles for a theology for a just peace. We invited reflection, amendment, and enrichment to our provisional list of principles. Here I have reorganized the list into separate categories for purposes of this discussion.

Scriptural Roots
♦ Peacemaking is a sacred calling of the gospel, especially blessed by God, making us evangelists of *shalom*—peace that is overflowing with justice, compassion, and well-being.
♦ Perfect peace is beyond human power; it is that grace that is the whole of God's love in action. For Christians, that grace is ultimately the gift of God through Jesus Christ.

Just Governance
♦ Government is a natural institution of human community in God's creation as well as a requirement for the restraint of human evil.
♦ Every policy of government must be an act of justice and must be measured by its impact on the poor, the weak, and the oppressed—not only in our own nation but in all nations.
♦ Loyalty to one's own government is always subject to the transcendent loyalty that belongs to the Sovereign God alone. Such loyalty may be politically expressed either in support of or in opposition to current government policies.

World Order

◆ The transformation of our conflict-ridden nation-state system into a new world order of common security and interdependent institutions offers the only practical hope for enduring peace.

◆ No nation may presume the powers of ultimate judgment on the fate of other nations, even to their destruction.

Common Security

◆ Security is not only a legitimate concern but also an imperative responsibility of governments for the protection of life and well-being. But the security of which biblical prophets speak cannot be separated from the moral imperatives of justice and peace and the full range of basic human needs.

◆ Security is indivisible in a world threatened with total annihilation. Unilateral security is impossible in the nuclear age.

Just War

◆ Any just resort to coercive force must seek the restoration of peace with justice, refrain from directly attacking noncombatants, and avoid causing more harm than good.

◆ No just cause can warrant the waging of nuclear war or any use of nuclear weapons.

Just Peacemaking

◆ All Christians, pacifists and non-pacifists alike, ought to share a strong moral presumption against violence, killing, and warfare, seeking every possible means of peaceful conflict resolution.

◆ The gospel command to love enemies is more than a benevolent ideal; it is essential to our own well-being and even to our survival.

◆ Repentance is a prerequisite of reconciliation for individuals, groups, nations, and churches. The church's own implication in militarism, racism, sexism, and materialism requires a deeply penitent approach to peacemaking.

◆ Truthfulness is a necessary foundation of peacemaking. Lies tend to become tools of self-aggrandizement, weapons of hate, and acts of violence.

Human Rights and Environmental Rights

◆ Every person of every race and nation is a sacred being, made in God's image, entitled to full participation in the *shalom* of God's good creation—to life and peace, health and freedom.

◆ Peacemaking in the nuclear age, under the sovereignty of God, requires the defense of creation itself against possible assaults that may be rationalized in the name of national defense.

The Just-Peace Church
◆ The church of Jesus Christ, in the power and unity of the Holy Spirit, is called to serve as an alternative community to an alienated and fractured world—a loving and peaceable international company of disciples transcending all governments, races, and ideologies; reaching out to all "enemies"; and ministering to all the victims of poverty and oppression.
◆ Ecumenism, in all the fullness of baptism and Eucharist, and in common life throughout all the earth, is the new synonym for peacemaking.[8]

CONFRONTING DOMINATION SYSTEMS

An experience with Walter Wink, a professor at Auburn University in New York, helped me to understand that action for a just peace is often an *exorcism*. While I have participated in demonstrations against war, oppression, and injustice for four decades, I have been hesitant to engage in civil disobedience. No doubt my hesitation stemmed in part from my own innate timidity, fear of conflict, and awe of authority. In part it came from a strong sense of the risk to social order that civil disobedience involves or apprehension about the unpredictable, and perhaps escalating, slide toward anarchy. Too often employed, it loses its impact.

My first direct experience of civil disobedience occurred as I attended Society of Friends meetings in Cambridge, Massachusetts, during seminary days at Boston University. In each meeting young people who had been arrested during peace demonstrations would come to report on their activities. They were hailed as heroes. I could not overcome a strong sense of the futility of these tiny bands of dissidents struggling against massive forces of militarism in the culture. It all seemed so self-defeating. If one wished to influence public policy, an act so obviously unproductive, so easily stereotyped and ridiculed by the majority culture was certainly the wrong way to go about it. Civil disobedience is politically counterproductive, I thought.

But Walter Wink changed my thinking. We were arrested together for praying at the White House. This was the second time I had been arrested in demonstrating against the apartheid system in South Africa. The first time, as I have related, was a rather painless experience with the police, the court, and the community cheering us on. It is not so pleasant to be arrested at the White House. The Washington Park police are rather zealous to convince demonstrators to stay away. First, they secured our hands behind our backs with plastic handcuffs, which have the admirable trait of tightening as you struggle to ease them. The police left us bound on a bus for two-and-a-half hours, then brought us into the police station, handcuffed us to a long brass rail for another hour, fingerprinted and photographed us, then locked us into tiny cells to contemplate our sins. When we were released, we found ourselves miles away from the inner city, with no public transportation to take us back.

It was while sitting handcuffed on the bus that Walter Wink patiently explained to me that an act of civil disobedience is not primarily a political act, although it may issue in political change. It is an exorcism! It is a naming of the demons, the first step toward exposing them and stripping away their power to deceive, as Jesus revealed.

I was aware that Wink had spent much of his career writing a trilogy of books on naming, unmasking, and engaging the "principalities and powers" described in the Scriptures. Having read some of his work, I began to take seriously the biblical insights into the demonic as the inner spirit of cruel systems of injustice, oppression, war, and ecological rapaciousness.

Through years of comprehensive scholarship, Wink had become convinced that we need not see the demonic as "an order of angelic beings in heaven, or as demons flapping about in the sky." He concludes:

> My thesis is that what people in the world of the Bible experienced and called "Principalities and Powers" was in fact real. They were discerning the actual spirituality at the center of the political, economic, and cultural institutions of their day. The spiritual aspect of the Powers is not simply a "personification" of institutional qualities. . . . On the contrary, the spirituality of an institution exists as a real aspect of the institution even when it is not perceived as such. Institutions have an actual spiritual ethos, and we neglect this aspect of institutional life to our peril.[9]

The ancients intuited the evil in the "diseased spirituality" of an institution or state, such as the cruel and oppressive Roman Empire, and projected it out in personified or visualized form onto the "screen of the universe" as spiritual beings or forces living in the heavens. Reading the cosmos through the lens of the scientific ethos, we are no longer willing to give credence to demons in the sky. Yet this projection does not falsify reality:

> The demons projected onto the screen of the cosmos really are demonic, and play havoc with humanity; only they are not up there but over there, in the socio-spiritual entities that make up the one-and-only real world. Thus the New Testament insists that demons can have no effect unless they are able to embody themselves in people (Mark 1:21-28; Matt. 12:43-45; Luke 11:24-26), or pigs (Mark 5:1-10), or political systems (Revelation 12-13).[10]

Now I began to understand my conversations with the Ayatollah Khomeini and other religious and political leaders in Iran. It sounded bizarre to hear them speak of America as the "Great Satan." Venerating the Hebrew Scriptures even as we do, it was logical for the Iranians to use the language of the Jews and early Christians to personify as Satan the demonic spirituality of oppressive and cruel political and economic systems.

JUSTICE, PEACE, AND THE INTEGRITY OF CREATION

In the study *In Defense of Creation*, the Council of Bishops celebrated the growing strength of the ecumenical movement, the unification of divided churches, partnerships to address issues of peace and justice, and bilateral dialogues across lines of faith. We praised God for the World Council of Churches, which allowed the churches of the then Soviet Union to speak on many issues in unity with those in the United States and other countries. We called upon United Methodists to pray for our Christian brothers and sisters in the Soviet Union, to study Russian religious life, and to support ecumenical exchanges with Russian churches. Having led several such delegations to the Soviet Union and encouraged a series of youth visits from Alabama and the Northeastern Jurisdiction, I learned of the rich potential for reconciliation in such exchanges. I keep in my study the simple declaration: "A modest proposal for peace: let the Christians of the world agree they will not kill each other!"

It was in this spirit that more than a thousand of us gathered in Seoul, Korea, in March 1990 for the World Council of Churches' Consultation on Justice, Peace, and the Integrity of Creation. We were Protestant and Orthodox Christians from around the world, with participant observers from the Roman Catholic Church and Buddhism. We came together under the mandate defined in these words: "We are living between the flood and the rainbow: between the threats to life on the one side and God's promise for a new earth and a new heaven on the other. That is why we have gathered in Seoul to covenant for justice, peace, and the integrity of creation."

As early as 1983, the Sixth Assembly of the World Council had issued an invitation to its member churches to come to Vancouver "to engage . . . in a conciliar process of mutual commitment to justice, peace, and the integrity of creation." This theme has run as a guiding force in the world ecumenical movement since that time.

In Seoul we covenanted under the conviction that these three critical global issues are organically interrelated:

Justice, peace and the integrity of creation are distinct but inter-related ways of referring to the same fundamental reality: the goodness and wholeness of life intended by the will of the God of the covenant. This means life in right relationship with God, life in fulfilling relationships among human beings and between human communities, and life in harmonious relationships with the whole of creation. This is the eschatological vision that the Hebrew Bible calls *shalom*—a vision that is exemplified in Hosea 2:18-19, 21-23.[11]

Christians, along with those of other faiths, are locked into one coherent struggle for life against demonic systems of immense power. I have come to label these systems as hunger-making, war-making, and desert-making systems. As I wrote the Episcopal Address to the 1992 General Conference, my colleagues on the Council of Bishops agreed that we should use those terms to suggest important missional priorities facing the Christian community today. We summarized them as follows:

Hunger-making Systems. "Most of the human family lives in abject poverty, one failed monsoon away from catastrophe. . . . We must struggle to combat the root causes of global poverty. They are an affront to the God of justice and a challenge to the conscience of every Christian. Only the faithful exercise of our political ministry can challenge those demonic systems."

War-making Systems. "The militarization of the nations of the world is one of the tragedies of our time. Great-power struggles have been played out over the backs of the poor. Many poor nations spend more on the military than on development. Much of the military equipment they buy is utilized to war against their own people. The debt crisis in nation after nation is often related to the militarization of their societies. . . . We now know that the only security is common security. The 'new world order' will not emerge from the end of a gun. It demands an entire change of hearts and minds, a transformation of values, a new resolve to unite persons of good will all over the world to drive the hostile, alien presence from the earth. The military-industrial-scientific-academic-media complexes in all their manifestations must be starved into weak and withered shadows of their former selves."

Desert-making Systems. "A rising chorus of concern from the scientists has called our attention to the emerging environmental crisis. As we hear their warning that atmospheric warming might turn vast fertile areas of the planet into deserts, we recall again the words attributed to Chief Seattle: 'Your appetite will devour the earth and leave behind only a desert!' . . . We know now that the concern for the integrity of creation must be joined to the struggle for peace with justice. Hunger-making systems force the poor to denude their environment, 'eating their future' in the struggle to survive. The fate of the poor and the fate of the planet are interwoven. Militarization and state terrorism increase as the poor organize to free themselves from exploitation. The world's armed forces are a terrible polluter, and war lays waste the earth in a macabre dance of death. Now we know: we will have no peace on the earth until we have peace with the earth. We will have no peace on or with the earth until the people of the earth live together in the harmony of a just social order."

OUR BIBLICAL MANDATE

All human beings are born free and equal in dignity and rights. (*Universal Declaration*)

> So God created humankind in his image,
>> in the image of God he created them;
>> male and female he created them. (Gen. 1:27)

> The rich and the poor have this in common:
>> the LORD is the maker of them all. (Prov. 22:2)

> Then Peter began to speak to them: "I truly understand that God shows no partiality, but in every nation anyone who fears him and does what is right is acceptable to him. You know the message he sent to the people of Israel, preaching peace by Jesus Christ—he is Lord of all." (Acts 10:34-36)

> There is no longer Jew or Greek, there is no longer slave or free, there is no longer male and female; for all of you are one in Christ Jesus. (Gal. 3:28)

All human beings have the right to life, liberty, and security of person. (*Universal Declaration*)

> They shall build houses and inhabit them;
>> they shall plant vineyards and eat their fruit.
> They shall not build and another inhabit;
>> they shall not plant and another eat;
> for like the days of a tree shall
>> the days of my people be,
>> and my chosen shall long enjoy
>>> the work of their hands.
> They shall not labor in vain,
>> or bear children for calamity;
> for they shall be offspring blessed by the LORD—
> and their descendants as well.
> Before they call I will answer,
>> while they are yet speaking I will hear.
> The wolf and the lamb shall feed together,
>> the lion shall eat straw like the ox;
>> but the serpent—its food shall be dust!
> They shall not hurt or destroy
>> on all my holy mountain,
>>> says the LORD.
> (Isa. 65:21-25)

"The Spirit of the Lord is upon me,
   because he has anointed me
      to bring good news to the poor.
He has sent me to proclaim release to the captives
   and recovery of sight to the blind,
      to let the oppressed go free,
to proclaim the year of the Lord's favor." (Luke 4:18-19)

NOTES

1. See Mia Adjali and Deborah Storms, *The Community of Nations* (New York: Friendship Press, 1995), p. 11.

2. *The Book of Resolutions of The United Methodist Church* (Nashville: The United Methodist Publishing House, 1996), p. 48.

3. *In Defense of Creation: The Nuclear Crisis and a Just Peace*, Foundation Document of the United Methodist Council of Bishops (Nashville: Graded Press, 1986), p. 6.

4. *Book of Resolutions*, p. 51.

5. *In Defense of Creation*, p. 15.

6. Ibid, p. 14.

7. Ibid., p. 15.

8. Adapted from ibid., pp. 36-37.

9. Walter Wink, *Engaging the Powers* (Minneapolis: Fortress Press, 1992), p. 6.

10. Ibid., p. 8.

11. Second Draft Document, *Justice, Peace, and the Integrity of Creation*, World Council of Churches, 1990.

Study Guide

Questions for Reflection

What are the implications for human rights in the biblical revelation "created in the image of God"?

How was the ecumenical community instrumental in shaping the *Universal Declaration of Human Rights?*

What are some of the current violations of human rights in your local community? the nation? the international arena?

Do you agree that "war is incompatible with the teachings and example of Christ"?

What are some important guiding principles for a theology of a just peace?

Do you believe that the demonic is not "up there" in the cosmos, but "out there" in the inner spirituality of systems of domination, exploitation, and oppression?

How may we resist principalities and powers that have become demonic in character?

Suggestions for Local Church Study/Action

◆ Form a study/action group using *The Community of Nations,* by Mia Adjali and Deborah Storms, and the *Study Guide to the United Nations,* written by Mia Adjali.

◆ Join the regional chapter of Amnesty International and respond faithfully to calls to protest violations of human rights as they come in the mail. Write to Amnesty International of the U.S.A., 304 West 58th Street, New York, NY 10019.

◆ Get on the mailing list of Human Rights Watch, the umbrella organization that monitors and reports on human rights abuses around the world and tries to influence U.S. foreign policy. Write to Human Rights Watch, 485 Fifth Avenue, New York, NY 10017.

◆ Organize a seminar for a local group in New York and Washington, concentrating on current issues in human rights. Contact the United Methodist Seminar on National and International Affairs at the Church Center for the United Nations, 777 UN Plaza, New York, NY 10017 (212-682-3633) or The Methodist Building, 100 Maryland Ave., Washington, D.C. (202-488-5600).

◆ Join the local chapter of the United Nations Association of the USA, an organization responsible for educating the public and coordinating action for the UN. Write to the United Nations Association, 801 2nd Ave., New York, NY 10017 (212-907-1300; fax: 212-682-9185).

◆ Be alert to local human rights abuses, with special attention to the most vulnerable persons in your community, such as women and children, racial/ethnic groups, and the poor. Join local coalitions that may be advocating for the rights of the oppressed in your midst.

Selected Resources

Video
The UN: Earth's Hope—a 28-minute video celebrating the story of the UN, along with the formative and supportive role of the churches. Write to the Church Center for the United Nations, 777 UN Plaza, New York, NY 10017.

In Defense of Creation—a half-hour program on the preparation of the nuclear study *In Defense of Creation,* by the Council of Bishops of The United Methodist Church. Many local churches and United Methodist Annual Conference audiovisual libraries have this resource available.

Books

On Human Rights

The Community of Nations, Mia Adjali and Deborah Storms (New York: Friendship Press, 1995)—an excellent resource for local church study. Chapters focus on peacekeeping, human rights, the environment and sustainable development, women, children, and health—issues of mutual concern to the UN and Christians. Contains basic information about UN membership, structure, history, peacekeeping operations, world conferences and special observances, and achievements related to the status of women. Order along with the study guide from Friendship Press, P.O. Box 37844, Cincinnati, OH 45222-0844 (513-948-8733).

Human Rights and the Politics of Terror, Gary E. McCuen (GEM Publications, 1995)—a collection of brief articles on current crises in human rights and methods of humanitarian intervention. Contains chapters on torture, political murder and the disappeared, rights of Native Americans, the world's indigenous peoples, rape and sexual abuse, and genocide in Bosnia. It is set up as a series of debates to encourage discussion. Order from GEM Publications Inc., 411 Mallalieu Drive, Hudson, WI 54016 (715-386-7113).

Taking a Stand Against Human Rights Abuses, Michael Kronenwetter (Franklin Watts, N.Y., 1990)—an overview of the history of human rights activism and the current status of human rights in the world. The emphasis is on what you can do to combat human rights abuses. Practical suggestions on methods of organization and action are offered. It quotes an Amnesty International publication: "The only real protection for human rights is people. People who speak out when they see human rights being violated."

Freedom of Religion and Belief, Kevin Boyle and Juliet Sheen (London: Roultedge, 1997)—this is the first report of its kind to offer a detailed and impartial account of how the right to hold beliefs is understood, protected, or denied throughout the world. It exposes persecution and discrimination in virtually all regions of the world.

Human Rights in the World Community, Richard Pierre, Claude Weston, and Burns H. Weston (Philadelphia: University of Pennsylvania Press, 1992)—for advanced study, this volume offers a collection of excellent articles on the theory and practice of human rights and the remedies of wrongs. Targeted toward academic audiences, it aims to disseminate knowledge about human rights. Some of the leading advocates and scholars in the field analyze a complex subject in a readable style.

Amnesty International Report 1997 (London: Amnesty International Publications, 1997)—this report exposes some of the human rights violations that force refugees to seek asylum in countries other than their own. It documents abuses in 151 countries and challenges governments to protect their people from human rights abuses.

The Human Rights Reader, ed. Micheline R. Ishay (New York: Routledge, 1997)—the essays in this volume trace the debate over human rights back to its biblical origins by including passages from the Old and New Testaments, the Koran, and early Buddhist writings. Contemporary issues are discussed, such as women's rights, the rights of gays and lesbians, and the question of humanitarian intervention.

Paradox and Promise in Human Rights, Peggy Billings (New York: Friendship Press, 1977)—the study book deals with the post World War II scene in the U.S. and Canada, as well as worldwide. The author uses Korea as a case history. The role of Christians as world citizens and in relation to the UN is defined. Mia Adjali wrote the accompanying study guide, entitled *Of Life and Hope: Toward Effective Witness in Human Rights* (also available from Friendship Press).

For a Just Peace

In Defense of Creation (Nashville: Graded Press, 1986)—the study of the nuclear crisis by the Council of Bishops of The United Methodist Church. No longer in print, it can be found in many local church libraries and pastors' studies.

Just Peacemaking, Glen H. Stassen (Louisville: Westminster/John Knox Press, 1989)—an excellent guide to peacemaking, based on recent biblical interpretation, the experiences of people who live in the face of oppression, Christian ethicists, and activists. The author's personal involvement in the liberation struggles in Eastern Europe that broke the back of Communist oppression enriches the work.

A Just Peace Church, ed. Susan B. Thistlethwaite (New York: United Church Press, 1986)—a theological, political, and programmatic guide to becoming a peacemaking church. Prepared for the United Church of Christ, it offers valuable guidance to the achievement of a just peace. It expresses the hope that we might put as much effort into defining a just peace as we have done in the past in defining a just war. In a world facing a new scale of global destructiveness, war has become dysfunctional.

On Domination Systems

Engaging the Powers, Walter Wink (Minneapolis: Fortress Press, 1992)—the third in a series on domination systems, this book has been hailed as one of the most important theological works to emerge in a generation. A provocative and insightful Bible study, it examines current myths of "redemptive violence" and economic and social exploitation as examples of the "principalities and powers" highlighted in the New Testament. The way of creative nonviolence is illuminated as the means for the transformation of the powers and of modern society.

Life in Its Fullness: The Word of God and Human Rights—produced for the NCCC by the American Bible Society, New York, this is a meditation book with biblical resources, giving understanding to human rights. Order from the American Bible Society, 1865 Broadway, New York, NY 10023.

Chapter 2

Resisting Hunger-Making Systems: Poverty

Everyone has the right to work, to free choice of employment, to just and favorable conditions of work and to protection against unemployment.

—The Universal Declaration of Human Rights

Every policy of government must be an act of justice and must be measured by its impact on the poor, the weak, and the oppressed.

—In Defense of Creation

The people of Mozambique have no medicine! Can we take some to them?" I was in my office as bishop of New York. The call came from an amazing Harlem physician, Dr. Saundra Shepherd. She had been talking with UN officials and learned of the desperate situation in a country plagued by five years of drought and years of guerrilla attacks. Renamo, "bandits," were using the arms shipped in by their allies, the apartheid government of South Africa. Their brutal campaign of slaughter and intimidation had sent hundreds of thousands of people fleeing for their lives. Food production was impossible. A starving people had no medicines to treat hunger-related diseases. Dr. Shepherd embodied the spirit of compassion so graphically described by Jesus in Matthew 25: "The people are hungry? Take food. The people are thirsty? Bring some water." The people of Mozambique needed medicine. Dr. Shepherd knew where she could get medicine at bargain-basement prices.

We decided to make an appeal to the New York Annual Conference. We sent out a letter inviting our congregations to participate in an errand of mercy. The people immediately responded with over $40,000. With those funds we were able to put together 27 old suitcases filled with $300,000 worth of medicines, some donated and some purchased at discounted prices. A delegation of us hand-delivered them, shuttling them up-country to our hospital in Chicuque in a Mission Aviation Fellowship plane. We were moved as the people told us over and over again, "We were in terrible need of medicine. But most of all we are so grateful that you came from halfway around the world to greet us. It means so much to us that our Christian brothers and sisters care."

Meeting with the regional authorities, we learned that the churches of the world were keeping hundreds of thousands of people alive during years of guerrilla warfare and terrible drought. Communist government officials told us that Christian generosity had transformed their attitudes toward church people. They allowed our churches and institutions to reopen. We arrived at the church on the hospital grounds in Chicuque just in time to witness a glorious celebration. The people came from miles around, filling the church and surrounding grounds. The United Methodist Women gathered for a district rally. Many had walked as long as nine days to get there, sleeping in the bush by night for fear of the guerrillas. As they knelt at the altar, I noticed that most had no shoes; some had pieces of old tires strapped to their feet. Even today I cannot listen to our recording of their dance processional and inspired singing without having tears come to my eyes.

THE POOR OF THE WORLD

Most of the human family lives in abject poverty, one failed monsoon or military adventure away from catastrophe. The weakest, women and children, suffer the most in every place around the world. More than 1.2 billion people worldwide do not get enough to eat to sustain active and healthy lives. Every year 40 million people die from hunger and hunger-related diseases.

It is very difficult to empathize with the poor of the earth without having seen their faces. I have seen their faces. In India, they were the barefoot children playing alongside open sewers in the biggest slum in the world, Bombay. They were the women and children in refugee camps in Zimbabwe and Sierra Leone, the children running when a clanging gong announced their one meal a day of rice and dried sardines, then going back to their classrooms under the trees. They were three little boys on the streets of Rio de Janiero, huddled together against the cold, still asleep as I left for the Earth Summit sessions. I must not forget the tiny, crowded classroom in Bangladesh where the children had no seats, books, or writing implements, shouting out their lessons in a loud voice to let the world know they are alive. The teacher showed us one boy who was sitting in the classroom, silently going blind for lack of vitamin A. They caught him just in time. The children of the earth are everywhere beautiful, if they get enough to eat so that their little bellies are not distended and their bones protruding.

It should be easy for us to understand why Jesus loved the children of the earth—and loves them still. In his day, the "crowds," the "little ones," gathered around him everywhere. They were the landless poor of Palestine, marginalized and oppressed, "harried and helpless, driven and riven." His words of hope and his healing touch were manna in a dry and thirsty land. He broke bread with them in violation of the taboos of his culture. He promised them that God was bringing a new realm of salvation on earth, and it would be their inheritance.

I remember September 1990, a historic moment when seventy-one heads of state gathered in New York City, where I served as bishop. This largest gathering of heads of state in human history up to that time came to talk about the *children* of the earth. It is not unusual to hear of a summit gathering, but this was the United Nations World Summit for Children. For the first time, I learned that 14,000,000 precious children die on this globe every year—two silent holocausts. At least two-thirds die from diseases that could be prevented or cured at limited cost—fresh water, inoculations, rehydration salts, basic nutrition. I remember hearing the estimates of UN officials that if just 5 percent of the military burden carried by the human family could be focused on the right kinds of development, the children would not have to die.

At the World Summit for Children, Secretary General of the UN, Perez DeCuellar said, "*Poverty* is the main enemy of children." We have a new opportunity in this decade, he said. With the cold war over, we can now establish a world order that encompasses not only the maintenance of peace and security, but also the better management of the world's economic and social affairs. We spent billions of dollars to right an injustice in wealthy Kuwait. What are we willing to spend to seek justice for the poor and destitute of the world, the *ochlos* for whom Jesus lived and died?

The churches of the world continue to express the compassion of Jesus through their emergency relief programs. We are often ridiculed by those who believe our relief programs do no good, or even do more harm than good. A few years ago some of our churches withheld their mission funds because the *Reader's Digest* had published an article saying that we were Communist sympathizers. Why? We had sent tons of wheat to Vietnam. Checking into it, I learned that the wheat was turned into macaroni to feed hungry children in orphanages. Faced with such atrocious disinformation campaigns, for sixteen years as a bishop I took groups of leaders to observe our relief and development programs on three continents. I can testify that the combined efforts of UMCOR, Church World Service, Catholic Relief Services, Lutheran World Relief, and other agencies are keeping millions alive and improving the quality of life for millions more.

We are making a substantial contribution, not only through emergency relief, but also through creating models of integrated rural and urban development in country after country. Such programs earn us immense credibility when we advocate for the systemic changes required for preventing poverty and destitution. *Yet how often we neglect our advocacy role!*

We must learn to think about root causes of hunger and illness. Our compassion leads us to create health clinics, to send medicines and medical personnel to treat the sick. Yet the World Health Organization estimates that 80 percent of illness comes from malnutrition, polluted water, and poor sanitation. Cholera has spread in recent years in South America as well as in Nigeria and other African countries.

Cholera is a preventable disease of poverty, of poor sanitation, and of polluted water and food. Rehydration salts and pure water can prevent the spread of cholera today. A woman in Guatemala told us, "They invited everyone to a party to celebrate the new world order, and guess who came—cholera!" In Africa, AIDS came to the party. It is spreading like wildfire in central Africa, fueled by disrupted family life, poor sanitation, untreated infections, and weakened immune systems through inadequate nutrition and social chaos.

Clearly, the suffering of the poor is more than a medical or a nutritional problem. It is a justice problem. We must confront the death-dealing forces of exploitative economic and political systems that enrich the few at the expense of the many. *People's policies* make people poor and hungry—not the inability of the earth to provide food. Since people created those cruel policies, people can change them—and must change them.

Some observers are now saying that as apartheid was in South Africa, so the global capitalism is on a worldwide scale. The global economy is a legalized system to deprive much of the human family of the resources needed for life. A reverse Marshall Plan is at work on a global scale. The transfer of capital worth billions of dollars from the poor to the rich countries goes on year after year. The global economy is the story of "aid" that does not aid, of "development" that does not develop, of loans that impoverish the borrower, of unfair terms of trade. The global economy is a device to move the life-giving resources from the place in the world where they are most needed to the place in the world where they are least needed.

Austerity programs, so-called structural adjustment programs, forced on poor nations by the World Bank and the Interna-

> *The most devastating aspect of "structural adjustment" lending has been the transfer of resources from Africa to the developed countries in the form of debt repayment. Africa has established a "Marshall Plan" of its own out of its poverty. . . . In short, "structural adjustment" is nothing more than a substitute for gunboat diplomacy to enforce the unilateral will of the powerful Western nations. The overwhelming consensus among the poor in Africa today is that development, over the past 25 years, has been an instrument of social control. For these people, development has always meant the progressive modernization of their poverty. The absence of freedom, the sacrifice of culture, the loss of solidarity and self-reliance which I personally observed and experienced in many African countries, including my own, explains why a growing number of poor Africans beg: please do not develop us!*
>
> —Fantu Cheru

tional Monetary Fund, were supposed to solve the debt crisis and put those nations on the road to economic recovery. Instead, they have too often left the social safety nets in many countries in a shambles. Schools, clinics, and food subsidies have been cut back, as will be discussed later in this chapter.

Our Biblical Mandate

Whenever we speak or act on behalf of the poor, angry voices surface, charging that the church has no authority to speak on such matters. During the cold war years, we had to withstand a drum beat of attacks. They most often accused us of coming under the influence of Communist dogma. Ingenious terms like "Comsimp" or "pink fringe" were used to convince church people that we had been taken in by Soviet propaganda. To all such critics we responded that we were guided by the scriptural vision of *shalom*. *Shalom* is positive peace—harmony, wholeness, health, and well-being in all human relationships. In the covenant of *shalom*, there is no contradiction between justice and peace or between peace and security or between love and justice (Jer. 29:7).

Wherever we look in the Hebrew Scriptures, we see that God stands passionately and powerfully on the side of the oppressed of the world. The weak, the exploited, the marginalized have a special place in the heart of God:

> Do not rob the poor because they are poor,
> or crush the afflicted at the gate;
> for the LORD pleads their cause
> and despoils of life those who despoil them.
> (Prov 22:22-23)

> Ah, you who make iniquitous decrees,
> who write oppressive statutes,
> to turn aside the needy from justice
> and to rob the poor of my people of their right,
> that widows may be your spoil,
> and that you may make the orphans your prey!
> What will you do on the day of punishment,
> in that calamity that will come from far away?
> (Isa. 10:1-3)

Indeed, the very essence of God is justice and righteousness. No one knows God who does not know justice:

> Thus says the LORD: Do not let the wise boast in their wisdom, do not let the mighty boast in their might, do not let the wealthy boast in their wealth; but let those who boast boast in this, that they understand and know me, that I am the LORD; I act with

39

steadfast love, justice, and righteousness in the earth, for in these things I delight, says the LORD. (Jer. 9:23-4)

Jesus positioned himself in the tradition of the Hebrew prophets when he announced the heart of his ministry on earth:

"The Spirit of the Lord is upon me,
  because he has anointed me
    to bring good news to the poor.
He has sent me to proclaim
    release to the captives
  and recovery of sight to the blind,
    to let the oppressed go free,
to proclaim the year of the Lord's favor." (Luke 4:18-19)

To the Hebrew prophets' cry for justice, Jesus added compassion and the daily healing of persons who suffer from injustice. Throughout his ministry he modeled the truth that God's justice cannot be separated from God's peace and love and mercy. He revealed clearly the Hebrew understanding that righteousness goes beyond justice. It involves kindness, compassion, and mercy. God's concern for justice grows out of God's compassion and mercy.

Moreover, Jesus engaged in acts of civil disobedience. Again and again, his compassionate acts of healing were a direct public challenge to the laws that made persons hungry and ill. Jesus first harvested and ate a handful of grain on the sabbath, then healed a man whose right hand was withered—both unlawful acts, as his self-righteous critics were quick to point out. His healing in the synagogue was an act of civil disobedience, since only the scribes had authority there. His was a powerful witness to the priorities of God: to feed the hungry and to heal the sick. These are the primary demands of the law of God, the reward and incentive system in the reign of God to come (Matthew 25).

AFRICA: A CASE STUDY IN GLOBAL INJUSTICE

We were meeting in August 1995 in Nigeria with United Methodist leaders. Six of us from the General Board of Global Ministries of The United Methodist Church were consulting with thirty key Nigerian leaders. The Nigerian Annual Conference lay leader said, frustration in his voice, "We are building on sand when we construct churches, schools, and clinics while our society collapses around us!"

For four years (1992–96), I worked with the World Division of the General Board of Global Ministries on a program of study and action on African development. The experience has convinced me that the African continent, home to one in five persons on earth, is an important case study in global economic injustice. Focusing on sub-Saharan Africa in this chapter, we can document the powerful interlocking systems that threaten basic human rights. These systems operate in varying degrees throughout the globalized economy.

The decade of the 1980s was disastrous for most of the African continent. According to UN figures, infant mortality rates in Africa, a powerful index of human well-being, are now more than three times the rate for Southeast Asia and over double the rate for Latin America and the Caribbean. Real wages fell by 30 percent between 1980 and 1989, and unemployment quadrupled. A combination of apartheid, social unrest, and military adventures created 7 million refugees, 50 million disabled persons, and 35 million displaced people. The UN Social Summit in 1995 singled out Africa as the area of greatest human suffering. The continent deserves the concerted efforts of the international community to stop the hemorrhaging and to bring help and healing.

The churches of the West have a special interest in Africa. The United Methodist Church and its predecessor denominations have invested blood, prayers, and tears in Africa for over one hundred years. Our mission partnership has been inspiring and enriching for the entire Christianity community. Together we have built churches, hospitals, clinics, and schools. We have witnessed the emergence of outstanding African leaders. We have seen bodies healed, spirits inspired, Christian commitments in the millions. The Africa Church Growth and Development program has allowed us to share in a most remarkable and dynamic church-growth experience. Together we are creating a major university on the continent. Through the United Methodist Committee on Relief (UMCOR) and our Advance Special giving, working with the ecumenical Church World Service and other agencies, we have sustained lives during food emergencies and created development programs that have been models for others.

All too often we have been forced to stand by helplessly while the fruits of our labors were spoiled again and again by corrupt governments, social turmoil, and war. Schools and clinics must be built and rebuilt—and rebuilt again. We see clearly now what the Scriptures have taught since ancient times: Only justice and righteousness bring peace. Until the international community dismantles the systems that exploit the poor and powerless of the world, we will have no peace. As our Nigerian friend said, "We are building on sand!"

If the mission investments of our churches are to bear fruit, we must struggle to grow beyond a narrow relief mentality. We must learn to analyze some of the root causes of the African crisis and identify priorities in mission that focus on systemic justice. This chapter highlights some key elements of sustainable development in sub-Saharan Africa, where so much of our historic mission presence has been concentrated. The complex experience of the successful struggle against the apartheid system in South Africa and the unique development needs in North Africa deserve fuller discussion elsewhere.

At the White House Conference on Africa in 1994 we were told, "Do not surrender to Afro-pessimism!" With all of its current problems, Africa is rich in natural resources and blessed with peoples of amazing survival skills, spiritual resilience, and courage. Two questions focus the discussion in this section. This outline of some key elements of sustainable development in Africa is meant to stimulate evaluation of the mission of the churches in two arenas:

1. As church members, will we examine every facet of our ongoing ministries in Africa in terms of their contribution not only to the transformation of lives through the gospel, but also the social transformation required for long-term sustainable development?

2. Will we examine our consciences to see whether we are faithful stewards of our political ministry, organizing with others to help to shape United States public policy on behalf of peace, freedom, and justice in Africa?

The Challenge of Food Security

Africa is rich in natural resources. Most African countries rely mainly on agriculture and forest products, not only to feed their people, but also to earn foreign exchange to sustain urban populations and develop an industrial sector. Agriculture remains the mainstay of the continent's economy. It contributes nearly 40 percent of gross domestic product (GDP), 30 percent of exports, and 75 percent of employment. The African people, in spite of drought and war, increased food production by 43 percent in fifteen years. Yet a quarter of Africa's people do not get enough to eat.

What has gone wrong? Government policies have often discriminated against farmers, making it unprofitable for them to grow more food. Environmental problems in some areas take their toll as poor people are forced to "eat their future" in order to survive. Poorly conceived "development projects" have done more harm than good, most often because African farmers were not consulted, their knowledge of land and forests ignored by outside development "experts." Civil strife and war have driven millions from their lands in Liberia, Sierra Leone, Angola, Mozambique, and other countries. Systemic poverty takes its toll, since poor people cannot pay the price farmers need to grow food, and no money is available to improve agriculture.

In addition, *bias against women* threatens food security in Africa. In rural Africa, 60-80 percent of food production, storage, and preparation, both in fields and forests, is done by women. Yet international "development" projects routinely ignore their productive wisdom. They take land and forests away from them to grow cash crops for export while denying them access to inputs and the technical

> *The evidence is overwhelming that, by ignoring women farmers [in Africa], the current thrust of agricultural policy . . . is to hamstring domestic food production. . . . It is clear that providing women with fair access to resources, and establishing policies that encourage domestic food production, would go a long way toward closing the growing gap in food security.*
>
> —*Worldwatch Paper #110,*
> a publication of the
> Worldwatch Institute

assistance offered to men. Women's agriculture is dismissed as the "informal sector," and is not even measured on the books.

Development experts are beginning to understand that the most effective way to stimulate food production is to sponsor small-scale self-help projects. They must employ appropriate technologies and farming methods that fit the local environment. Since women have for generations produced most of the food and fiber, their accumulated wisdom must be heard. The bleached bones of failed large-scale agricultural development projects litter the African landscape. Western "experts" with impressive credentials have again and again ignored local wisdom and left behind eroded fields and impoverished people. I have been privileged for two decades to travel with mission teams to visit our rural development programs. I am grateful to report that church-related projects offer the models Africa needs for the future.

The Challenge of Population Control

African leaders traditionally have believed that population explosion, a problem for Asia, has had no relevance to Africa's concerns. They are now awakening to the reality that most sub-Saharan African nations have the highest rate of population growth of any time in human history! At this rate, sub-Saharan Africa's population has doubled over the past 25 years and will double again in the next 25. While a number of African countries are actually underpopulated and population control measures are not a high priority, others, such as Nigeria, cannot long sustain the current rate of growth. Growth at this rate is already threatening food supplies.

Once again, gender bias plays a decisive role in the population crisis in Africa. Misguided development projects that discriminate against women *increase* their need to bear *more* children. When a woman's basic resources are taken away, she is actually likely to want more children to help her shoulder the increased workload. This is the *population trap.* Programs carried out in the name of development often increase women's dependence on children as a source of status and security. The UN Conference on Population and Development, (Cairo 1994) recommended strategies to empower women. If these strategies can be implemented, population problems, women's health-care concerns, women's and infant mortality rates will decline, and poverty will be alleviated. How can we face the God of justice if we continue to condemn five million African babies to die every year, when we know how to prevent it?

The Challenge of Sustainability

Environmental degradation across much of Africa is approaching catastrophic proportions. Life support systems are eroding rapidly throughout the continent. Although a continent of farmers, Africa is losing its ability to feed itself. In some countries, almost a quarter of the people are fed mainly with grain from abroad.

Even more alarming is the evidence that the prolonged drought from which much of Africa has suffered over the past two decades is caused by human activity. The rapid loss of forest cover, the fastest in the developing world, the deterioration of grasslands, and the degradation of soils is disturbing long-range rainfall patterns. Meteorologists warn of a cascading effect in which sustained overuse of eco-systems can set in motion changes that are self-reinforcing. Each stage of deterioration hastens the onset of the next. The disruption of self-regulating mechanisms in natural systems needed for human life is especially disastrous among populations of poor people who survive on subsistence agriculture.

The restoration of fertility to African soils is critically needed. The fragile soils of Africa cannot benefit from "green revolution" inputs of expensive fertilizers and insecticides. Only organic farming practices will succeed. Replanting African forests is essential if life-giving moisture is to be available for agriculture in future decades. Clearing land for farming and commercial logging is the greatest cause of deforestation. But the exploding demand for firewood is degrading Africa's remaining forests. Wood is Africa's primary fuel, and supplying it is the continent's largest industry.

The Challenge of Economic Growth

After three decades of improvement, the standard of living of the people of sub-Saharan Africa fell in the 1980s. Africans are poorer today than they were thirty years ago. Five of the largest African countries, Nigeria, Ethiopia, Zaire (now the Congo), Tanzania, and Kenya have experienced negative growth over the past decade. The debt burden increased from $18 billion to over $175 billion in fifteen years. Roads are falling apart, communications systems are deteriorating, and the small industrial base is stagnating. The human cost has been great, as schools and medical services have deteriorated and food has become scarce. What has happened?

We need to understand how bitter the colonial legacy has been in Africa. The economies of most of the countries are neo-colonial systems. While country after country achieved political independence in a remarkable historic development, most remain dependent economically. For a century, the development of the colonies was designed to benefit the colonial masters, not the majority of the African people. Roads, communications systems, and industries—indeed, the entire economic infrastructure—were built to sustain colonial exploitation of African resources and African people. It is not surprising that these facilities are decaying.

Moreover, Africa is caught in a commodity trade trap. African economies are built mainly upon mineral and agricultural exports. Prices of these commodities have been dropping rapidly, while interest rates on borrowed money have risen and the prices for essential imported goods are increasing. Everything Africa sells, it sells wholesale; almost everything it buys, it buys retail. The value added of processed goods goes to others. What solution does the World Bank propose for these problems? More of the same: increased exports of commodities to the world market.

Critics of IMF/World Bank policies say that their strategy of export-led development for Africa's problem is not only futile, but also cruel. "If you want access to foreign capital," African leaders are told, "you must trade more." This means that more resources must go into "tradeables" at the expense of "non-tradeables," which are the goods and services people need for survival. In the words of one observer, "The export-led strategy Africans have been obliged to adopt quite simply has not worked, does not work, cannot work."

The World Bank demands "structural adjustment" if African countries are to be eligible for foreign capital. Austerity programs are supposed to assure sustainable development. Their effect has been the opposite. African governments have been forced to impoverish poor and working people and to cut off support to health services and schools. Nutritional and health standards have deteriorated. Babies are dying because of impersonal bureau-

Is anybody interested in justice? What is the truth about Africa's international debt? Perhaps when the truth around these financial transactions, which have economically crippled Africa, is finally exposed we shall be as shocked as the world was when we comprehended the atrocities of the Slave Trade or the Holocaust. And we shall again wonder aloud, "How can there be so much cruelty in the hearts of men?" For if it is a crime to kill half a million people in Rwanda, it should be a crime to steal millions of dollars, thereby causing the death of millions of innocent people through hunger, malnutrition, lack of adequate health care, and inflationary prices which make it impossible to provide the basic needs. Why is this not a crime?

—Wangari Maathai, at the White House Conference

45

cratic decisions made half a world away. Meanwhile, the debt burden has grown beyond the capacity of African governments to pay.

The Challenge of Stable Government

We need constantly to recall that the nation-states of sub-Saharan Africa are still in their infancy. Ghana, the first country to achieve independence in this century, is barely 35 years old. In our time we have lived through an amazing political transformation, as country after country has thrown off the colonial yoke.

Africans remind us that democracy in North America has taken 300 years of struggle and is still struggling to be born. The newly emerging African states began with severe handicaps. The colonial powers, however much they boasted of democracy at home, modeled autocratic rule in Africa. Human rights were never extended to the people of Africa. Most colonial powers left the African people, if not totally illiterate, certainly unskilled in nation building. Under colonial domination, Africans struggled to retain as much of their traditional norms and means of local and regional governance as possible, cherishing a strong social contract among their own ethnic peoples. Central government was seen as an alien and often brutal force. Even after achieving independence, African people often view central government as a potentially disastrous intruder, like fire or drought. An intensive program of development and modernization requires political stability, which in turn requires a nationwide political consensus. This consensus has yet to be built in a number of countries. The result is civil strife and, in some cases, civil war.

The Challenge of Militarism

The cold war is not over in Africa. The great power struggle left a legacy of weapons caches, as the industrial powers armed their surrogate forces in the attempt to control sections of the continent. From Mozambique to Angola to Zaire the East/West conflict contributed to the destabilization of nations. The tragic situation in Somalia reveals the end product of the logic of war making. It is illuminating that for decades Somalia was second only to Iraq in the proportion of GNP spent on armaments. Africa's armies have impoverished the people and suppressed and silenced the very ones who must pay for them.

The cold war continues in Africa in other important respects. Arms left over from the great power struggle are streaming into the developing nations at discount prices. Hundreds of thousands of land mines left over from recent wars are killing and maiming women and children. Powerful military establishments have been left in place. Many African leaders were trained in military academies of the superpowers, came into power at the point of a gun, and assume that the road to power and affluence is armed struggle.

One legacy of colonialism is the assumption that the purpose of state power is to exploit the wealth of the people and that military force is the way to achieve it. Military force and the predatory accumulation of wealth are interrelated in much of Africa today. The United States, as the leading arms merchant of the world, can play a vital role in the demilitarization of African society. Pressure for international agreements to curb the arms race could mean life instead of death for millions of Africans. The arms trade contributes to the hunger of millions and to the creation of large numbers of refugees. It blocks development by taking scarce financial resources away from increasing the skills of the people through education, health, and jobs programs.

The Challenge of Human Development

"There can be no human development without people being alive, healthy, knowledgeable and able to make a decent living." Why should it have taken so long for otherwise intelligent people to understand this observation from the UN Development Program?

The World Summit for Children, which met at the UN in 1992, registered a growing international consensus: *Human development* must be the central objective and focus of the development

> *The leaders of an emergent African nation are charged with accomplishing at least four Herculean tasks in their lifetime: First, to force the bonds of unity and nationhood, and to foster wider loyalties beyond parochial, tribal or regional confines. Second, to convert a subsistence economy into a modern cash economy without unleashing social turbulence and economic chaos. Third, to industrialize the country and to introduce a sophisticated system of agriculture. Fourth, to erase poverty, disease and illiteracy, raise the standard of living of the people, and in short create a modern state with all its paraphernalia. The ex-President of Ghana, Kwame Nkrumah, proclaimed that he had to accomplish in ten years what the developed countries had achieved in a hundred.*
>
> —Samuel Asante, unpublished paper

process. The experience of the 1980s is that development schemes that force structural adjustment at the expense of human services have failed tragically and will fail in the future. A clear focus on the development of people, both as a means and, more important, as the aim of all development, is increasingly seen as essential to economic growth. This approach is particularly important in Africa, where the abundant natural resources can be made productive only if people have the chance to develop the full range of their capacities.

47

Education must be a key component of human development and, hence, of all sustainable development. Traveling through Africa in recent years, we are always besieged by young people who have no opportunity for higher education. "Can't you get us into the U.S. to study?" is their heart-felt plea. African governments have invested heavily in education, and progress has been made. Literacy rates have rises from 9 percent to 42 percent in three decades. The average working-age adult now has more than three years of education, compared to less than half a year in 1960. Now the schools are in crisis. A combination of fiscal restraints forced by international lending agencies, fast-growing populations of children, political instability, and violence have conspired to threaten the schools.

Health care is essential if Africa is to develop. If children come to school malnourished or ill, or are too sick to come at all, more than education is compromised. Africa's health-care system is in deep crisis. Visits to our own hospitals and clinics reveal dedicated doctors and nurses who valiantly struggle to offer minimal health care with little equipment and almost no modern medicines.

The AIDS crisis in some countries threatens to wipe out the fragile health-care advances made over thirty years. In Zaire, where barely 2,500 physicians care for millions, AIDS is spreading rapidly in an environment of poor sanitation, poor health, and family disintegration. Now 1.5 million to 2 million children are without fathers in sub-Saharan Africa, of which a majority have also lost their mother.[1] By the mid-1990s, 20 million Africans will be infected with HIV, striking young adults during their most productive years and decimating the economies of the countries hardest hit.

Nation-building skills must be developed through training if Africa is to develop. The strategic decision to offer a school of business administration at the new United Methodist Africa University follows a long-standing Methodist commitment to leader development on the continent. Methodists had a strong influence on the government of Great Britain in the last century by insisting on the right to train and educate Africans in community leadership. In the main, the colonial heritage is a bitter one. A dearth of management skills cemented dependence on transnational corporations. The authoritarian style of colonial rule prevented the development of attitudes, skills, and institutions that make democracy possible.

The experience of thirty years reveals that development emerges from the people. No amount of financial or technical assistance from the outside can suffice, although it is critically needed. *Africans must develop Africa, under the leadership of Africans trained in all of the skills needed for modern nation building.*

Faith development makes a critical contribution to the values needed if African nations are to thrive in the future. This is central to the mission and ministry of the fast-growing African churches. Its importance for sustainable development can be witnessed in the exuberant worship and shared pastoral care we have observed in congregations created by the African Church Growth and Development program. The moral and spiritual support and nurture of people surviving through crisis after crisis is witness to the resurrection power of the gospel.

The subtle but essential human qualities nurtured by the churches of Africa can be illustrated by a visit to North Shaba in Zaire. There we observed that U.S. AID was working closely with the United Methodist churches in integrated rural development, building roads, expanding air strips near our hospitals, and supporting agriculture projects. We were able to visit the AID staff in Lubumbashi. They told us, "We work with the churches because there we find honest people who care about life in the villages, and who are organized into accountable structures. We know they will get the job done."

The Challenge of Rethinking Development Strategies

Conventional development strategies have simply not worked well in much of Africa. Alternative development strategies in Africa must involve the combination of empowerment, capacity building, growth, and equity. Characteristics must include self-sufficiency, ecological integrity, and a post-patriarchal culture. In short, development must respond to the needs of the people. This social and political process can be achieved only on the basis of people's participation in organization and decision making at all levels. It cannot be achieved by the narrow fiscal and monetary policies of the IMF/World Bank.

The important Steering Committee of African NGOs declared that "the way out of the present crisis lies fundamentally with the people of Africa themselves who must seize the initiative to determine their own destiny." The ten-point strategy the committee prepared in 1986 for the UN Special Session on Africa is a blueprint for a new future for Africa. In brief, it demands that the African people expose the inequities in the global economy and demand full democratic participation in decisions affecting their lives. They must demand a fair and just return in international marketing arrangements. All development programs must meet the needs of the ordinary African people, not foreign powers or their African cronies. The people of Africa must democratically decide their own development priorities, meeting the needs of the people first. Women, who produce most of the food in Africa, must participate fully in all decisions made about agriculture. A thorough democratization of the entire society requires protection of human rights and liberties. People must have full freedom to express themselves politically, to form associations and trade unions, to participate in all political activities without fear of repression, and to choose their own leaders.[2]

THE GLOBAL ECONOMY: AN INDICTMENT

Can we point to some of the policies that perpetuate the growing division between wealthy minorities and the teeming millions of the poor? The causes are many and varied, but I believe it is important to learn all we can about some of the mechanisms of economic exploitation. It is no longer news that a rapidly expanding web of mega-corporations links our world. Modern electronic communications allow them to make and implement in an instant decisions that reverberate around the world. As I write this, the stock markets in Asia are being watched nervously to assess the impact of their instability on the rest of the world. The cost of rescuing economies once hailed as global wonders is expected to run into the billions. No doubt, economic globalization has given millions of people higher living standards, better job opportunities, and a cornucopia of products at lower cost. It has also widened the gap between the rich and the poor and left people hungry in the developing nations. What is happening?

Global Capitalization Is Creating "Dessert and Fruit-Cocktail" Economies

In discussing the development crisis in Africa, we have seen how development programs that were supposedly designed to help poor people end up marginalizing them. They have created "dessert and fruit-cocktail" economies, in which productive land is taken out of food production for local people in order to grow luxury products for the wealthy. These programs put the poor to work, producing things they cannot buy and buying things they cannot produce.

My own decision to commit myself to witness and action on international capitalism took place in 1979–80, when I was pulled into the Iran hostage crisis. It was a dangerous time. A group of revolutionary students was holding the U.S. embassy and its personnel hostage in Teheran. It was an act designed to render the United States helpless to stifle the ongoing revolution. Instead, it infuriated the American people. The "helpless giant" syndrome, reinforced by the media, was making it difficult for President Jimmy Carter to continue a policy of restraint. An escalating military confrontation with the Soviet Union, which had long claimed sovereignty over northern Iran, seemed imminent. Even Senator Barry Goldwater, long seen as a "hawk," warned against military intervention.

In the midst of such turmoil, I was asked to join a delegation to travel to Ghom to take a Christmas message of peace to the Ayatollah Khomeini, who had sent a Christmas message to the Christians of the world. Ten days of travel in Iran followed, as we interviewed leading religious, political, and academic leaders. In June 1980, I returned to hand-deliver mail to the hostages, who were scattered into safe houses around the country following an aborted rescue attempt. This allowed two weeks more of interviews with Iranian leaders, including President Bani Sadr and his staff, and some business leaders. Whatever else happened to cause the nervous breakdown of a nation, I became convinced that misguided development programs played a major role.

So-called agricultural development forced hundreds of thousands of farmers off the land and into urban slums. A self-sufficient country was importing 90 percent of its grain fifteen years later. Five million people fled into the worst slum in the world. South Teheran had the highest drug abuse rate anywhere on the globe. We saw people living in caves and raw sewage running in the streets. Meanwhile, multinational corporations exploited the cheap labor of the desperate migrants in assembly plants, often paying a dollar a day. The people were producing goods for export, goods they could not buy. To compound the unrest, the arms merchants of the world, with the help of the Pentagon, had poured billions of dollars worth of armaments into the country.

Someone remarked that the Iranian revolution was revolution by cassette tape. While in Paris, Bani Sadr, himself a noted economist, was smuggling lectures into the Iranian villages on audiotapes. The people would gather on Friday afternoons in thousands of mosques across the country. There they were learning that their development capital was hemorrhaging. Their country was being de-developed by Western powers. It is said that people revolt under revolting conditions. The people could see that they needed to move quickly to regain political control of their economy, or they would be doomed to a thousand years of poverty when their oil was exhausted.

At the 1980 General Conference, I was asked to speak on the Iranian crisis. The conference asked me to head a delegation to the White House to offer our support for continuing restraint. We were convinced that the Iranian people had legitimate complaints. Unlike many Third World revolutions, which involve only a shift in power elites, the Iranian people were completely mobilized behind the revolution. Military intervention could cost 500,000 lives or more. Following the White House visit, Mia Adjali enabled us to visit with Monsour Farhang, the UN Ambassador from Iran, himself a noted international scholar. I said that I had read the UN figures that pointed to Iran as a case *par excellence* of effective development. Their gross national product had increased at an impressive rate over several years. Ambassador Farhang replied, "The economists who talk that way are like the proud parents of a new baby. Every day they put the baby on the scales and remark at its amazing growth. They do not notice that the baby is growing grotesquely. One arm is extending out of proportion to the other. The head is so huge that the baby cannot hold it up. They are so proud they cannot believe they have given birth to a mutant."

Unjust economic systems are disrupting nations, destroying cultures, and rendering thousands destitute. The gods did not ordain these systems. They were created by human beings; therefore, they are subject to human reform. Modern warfare is a crime against humanity, a crime against nature, and a blasphemy to God. Death through international finance is not a lesser evil.

Multinational Corporations Can Buy and Sell Nations

With the massive and growing power of corporations, the power of local and national governments is diminishing. Spanning national borders, corporations have little interest in advancing national goals. Their objective is to grow, to expand profits and market share, and to create an environment free of regulations. What are the interests of local and national governments? To provide jobs for their people, to develop their economy, to ensure the rights of workers and consumers, and to protect the natural environment. Globalized companies routinely avoid government restrictions designed to accomplish these goals. They simply move production and capital to countries or localities with a more pliant government.

In the interests of global profit maximization, managers of investment portfolios develop ingenious ways of punishing corporations, governments, or even entire countries or regions. If returns weaken or restrictions on industry are attempted, they threaten to leave. If that fails, with a push of a button billions of dollars of investment capital can be transferred across the globe. Nothing is sacred. Loyalty to a community, a region, or a nation is ruthlessly withheld. As one observer remarked, "Now capital has wings!" Working people are rooted in communities, but capital has wings.

What happens to human rights when government elites cooperate as predatory corporations and investors exploit their people, bleed their natural resources and denude their environment? Political and civil rights are lost! With the loss of political rights, economic and social rights are gone. How can democracy survive when the wealth of corporations can force or bribe national leaders to sell out their own people? What good is the vote if elected officials cannot protect their people?

We see what happens to industrial workers when their right to organize is stripped from them. In the name of "free capital," the most primitive abuses of past centuries are revisited upon them. Decent working conditions, a living wage, job security—all are sacrificed on the altar of profit maximization. Those of us who lived through the Depression in the U.S.

> *An ideology based exclusively on competition and competitiveness necessarily leaves aside the poor, the downtrodden, the vulnerable and the unorganized: that is all of us, the poor of the South. . . . That is why there is a fundamental need for strategies aimed directly to combat poverty.*
>
> —Maria deLourdes Pintasilgo,
> in *Planeta Femea*, Brazilian
> Women's Coalition

remember the social unrest, the strikes, and the riots as working people struggled for a fair share of their productive labors. Each small gain was won at great cost, whether in wages, in hours on the job, in safe plants, or in health and pension benefits. Now "the tyranny of a rogue system" is ruthlessly snatching them away.

No Hiding Place Down Here

If we thought the workers in the wealthy nations would be immune to the abuses their corporations visit on the developing world, that illusion is fast disappearing in the cold light of reality. In the United States over the past two decades, the much-vaunted growth in income has gone to the wealthiest one percent at the top. Ownership of wealth has become even more concentrated. The gap between the highest and the lowest paid workers has widened dramatically. Three out of four workers have lost ground economically. With the rising power of corporations, working people have lost a comprehensive right: the right to self-determination, to control their own destiny.

According to a U.S. Census Bureau survey, American workers who lost their jobs in the compulsive down-sizing of the 1990–92 recession saw a 23 percent drop in wages when they went back to work. Meanwhile, corporate profits soared and the stock market rose. This was small comfort to workers, 80 percent of whose wages declined. Family incomes are now being maintained as two or more family members hold jobs. Now more than 75 percent of women with children under six are working outside the home. More and more jobs have been reduced to part-time or temporary status, with no benefits provided. As a result, 40 million Americans have no health insurance. Pension provisions are disappearing, and this at a time when the future of Social Security is on shaky ground. Meanwhile, under concerted corporate pressure, the Congress has been systematically dismantling the safety net for the poor. As I heard one journalist say, "They want it all now!"

As has been noted, global capitalization has systematically shifted power away from local communities and working people. Huge and interlocking global institutions are disconnected from the interests of the people they once served. The free-market dogma promised to put an end to high unemployment in industrial nations. Instead, we are witnessing a "race to the bottom" as wages and working conditions fall to the level of the most desperate.

Recent scandals in the apparel industry reveal the trend. Garment manufacturers have found it convenient to look the other way as the subcontractors who cut and sew the garments exploit their workers. Women and children often suffer the most. Inhuman labor practices are routine: hiring child labor, holding women captive to brutally long hours and dangerous working conditions, and cheating on over-time pay. Major manufacturers, such as Disney, The Gap, and Nike, are now under boycott action. It was recently reported that workers in the Nike plants in Vietnam are being paid eight cents a day!

Capital today flows at the touch of computer keys to the places on the globe that provide maximum profits to multinational corporations. In the interest of global profit maximization, small U.S. firms are identified for corporate giants to swallow up. They call them "cash cows." Firms making a reasonable profit are "milked" of their assets for investment in the sweatshops of northern Mexico, Manila, and Vietnam. A community that has thrived for decades suddenly loses its industry. The people are thrown out of work and the churches, businesses, schools, and medical services are strangled.

Meanwhile, if the exploited workers in the host country try to organize to demand better wages and working conditions, they are faced with police action. The factory may be closed and the entire operation moved to another country. "Nervous capital" leaves behind the scorched earth of impoverished communities and regions, both in the North and in the South.

David Korten has coined the phrase "corporate cannibalism." An orgy of mergers has allowed huge conglomerates to "capture and cannibalize" weaker market players. Unfortunately, the weaker market player "is often the firm that is committed to investing in the future; providing employees with secure, well-paying jobs; paying a fair share of local taxes; paying into a fully funded retirement trust fund; managing environmental resources responsibly; and otherwise managing for the long-term human interest."[3]

The corporate raiders who prey on stable companies often finance the entire operation with junk bonds. They establish receptacle corporations financed almost entirely with debt. The captured company is forced to pay the debt by raiding its pension funds, selling off profitable units, cutting employees and wages, or moving factories abroad. According to Korten, more than 2,000 recent cases are on record in which the new owners stripped a total of $21 billion from pension funds to pay the debts they had incurred to capture the firm.

Global Hunger-making Systems Are Desert-making Systems

Global corporations operate on a philosophy of escape. Their mobility allows them to run from national taxation, government regulations, and all of the controls that would make them socially responsible. Just as they race to the bottom in employment practices, so also they race to escape environmental regulations. What appears as amazing economic growth is revealed to be a threat to long-term human survival.

As this is being written, Congress has voted to deny President Clinton the fast-track provision that has allowed past administrations to negotiate international trade agreements that cannot be amended by congressional action. Commentators believe the congressional rebellion is a backlash against the North American Free Trade Agreement (NAFTA). The fears that led church groups to oppose NAFTA now appear to be justified. Some 200,000 American jobs have been lost as firms have fled to the *maquiladoras*, assembly plants on the Mexican side of the border. As expected, the Mexican government has held wages far below productivity increases. Working conditions are often atrocious, and workers are denied the right to form independent unions.

Just as the workers suffer, so also the earth suffers. Environmental regulations are routinely ignored in the *maquiladoras*. Extensive toxic dumping has polluted rivers and ground water. Serious health problems have emerged among the workers. Deformities among the babies born in the region are common. Fourteen-year-old children are reported to be working in the plants. They soon have problems with eyesight, allergies, and kidney problems.

North America is not free from corporate exploitation. Korten describes what happened when Pacific Lumber Company was taken over by corporate raider Charles Hurwitz. Pacific Lumber was one of the most environmentally sound timber companies in the U.S. It engaged in sustainable lumbering of its holdings of ancient redwoods on the California coast. Hurwitz immediately doubled the cutting rate of the thousand-year-old trees. They cynically dubbed the swath they cut "our wildlife-biologist study trail." To add insult to injury, they drained $55 million from the company's pension fund. The remainder of the fund was invested in the insurance company that financed the junk bonds used to buy Pacific Lumber. The insurance company soon failed.[4]

The United States has been a leader in setting environmental standards. This achievement has come at a cost. Every gain has been a struggle against free-market advocates. Today corporations engage in a constant battle against existing regulations. Their powerful lobbies, strengthened by generous donations to the election campaigns of members of Congress, try to gut environmental laws in the name of competitiveness. It should come as no surprise that American leadership is waning. Growing numbers of countries have surpassed us in the control of greenhouse gases. We are fast losing moral credibility as we try to obligate other countries to make sacrifices that we refuse to make.

Unregulated Capitalism Contains the Seeds of Its Own Demise

The classic contradiction within a free-running capitalist system is that it produces things it cannot sell. Driven by its internal logic of profit maximization, it creates market gluts, a drop in prices, and finally instability and possible collapse. Analysts such as David Korten and William Greider warn that "manic capital" is accelerating this trend beyond the danger point. A race for technological improvement has made possible great productive efficiency. Both products and the processes of making them are vastly improved. Each unit of production uses less energy, less labor, and less raw material input. The accelerating drive for globalization, the cut-throat competition for market share, and the race to build new factories in the developing world are seen as the formula for success.

The unfortunate result of all this is a growing surplus in productive capacity in sector after sector around the world. The nagging question is emerging: Who will buy all these goods? The global marketplace of consumers cannot absorb the excess supply. While too many cars are now chasing too few buyers, corporations race to out-do one another to expand production in the faltering economies of Asia. According to Greider, the same trends can be seen in steel, aircraft, chemicals, computers, consumer electronics, drugs, and tires. This growing gap between supply and demand will lead to "the storm of dislocations and shakeouts": "Whether these are described as restructuring or deindustrialization, more factories must be closed, more employees discarded, more production moved elsewhere."[5] A more ominous possibility is a decisive breakdown, an implosion of economic activity, similar to the Great Depression.

The Global Economy Employs False Standards of Success

Herman E. Daly is a past senior economist with the World Bank. He teamed up with John B. Cobb, Jr., a theologian who recently retired from Claremont Theological School in California. Together they wrote *For the Common Good*, in which they document a serious flaw in the global economy: The accounting assumptions that measure success and failure are grossly distorted.[6] What economists perceive to be growth is actually decline. While the U.S. economy is booming, according to accepted standards, it is actually becoming poorer. The index by which we measure growth, the Gross National Product (GNP), counts all economic transactions as good. It refuses to count the losses—damage to the environment in polluted water and air, lost topsoil, and holes in the ozone layer; the consumption of nonrenewable resources; the use of renewable resources beyond the capacity of the ecosystem to regenerate; deterioration in the quality of life. When the true costs of wealth-producing activity are measured, it is clear that the global system is "hurtling toward a wall" when economic expansion outruns the ecosystem that sustains it. Human ingenuity may postpone the day of reckoning, but it will come.[7]

The term *externalities*, used by corporate executives, is illuminating. Executives are rewarded for hiding the true costs of doing business. The human cost of substandard wages and massive layoffs, the toxic dumps and polluted streams, the costs of lobbying against government regulations—all are "externalized." They do not show on the corporate books. Who pays? The taxpayers who pick up the bill for environmental cleanup, the costs of restoring public health, and the care of those whose lives are ruined. Who pays? Future generations, who must try to survive in a world of depleted resources and a ruined biosphere. The world's most powerful decision makers convince themselves and others that they are creating wealth. In truth, they are enriching themselves at the expense of the people and the earth. They are lavishly rewarded for having made decisions that may lead to the destabilization and ultimate collapse of the entire system.

The Global Economy Reveals the Marks of a Domination System

In warning of principalities and powers, the early Christians were "discerning the actual spirituality at the center of the political, economic, and cultural institutions of their day."[8] They intuited the demonic inner spirituality of the repressive and cruel institutional life of the Roman Empire. The people suffered terribly from the taxation that bled their resources; the totalitarian reign, which stifled all attempts at reform; and the sacred emblems of the Romans, which violated their religious sensitivities. Their cosmology forced them to project the evil in the system in visionary form as a spiritual being residing in the heavens. Today we would withdraw the projections and see that the powerful and cruel spiritual forces we intuit emanate from the actual institutions that oppress us. The demons are not *up* there, but *over* there in the corporate entities and social mores that come under the control of exploitative power centers. They reflect the inner life of social and economic systems gone awry.

Even a brief analysis of the global economy reveals the characteristics of a domination system:

◆ Deviant values of greed, lust for power, and brutality become the operative forces driving the system. The result is a mayhem of inequality, injustice, and human deprivation. The universal longing for basic human rights is crushed. The political and civil rights that are the pillars of a just peace cannot thrive.
◆ The system takes on a life of its own, so powerful that it seems almost beyond control. Interlocking global corporations amass power indefinitely if no adequate forces are organized to curb them. The startling truth must be known: *No one is in charge of the global economy!* It is a free-running system. Korten is right: Corporations rule the world. With incredible new technologies and concentrated economic power, they devise ingenious ways of escaping the laws that are designed to protect human interests.
◆ Early Christians knew that demons disguise their true identities. They hide behind self-justifying mythologies that so permeate the culture that they seem to be absolute truth. Economic power today is being translated into control of media all over the world. Greider charges that corporate interests have wholly colonized television. The vivid images on the electronic screen paint an attractive picture of the good life. Greider quotes Paul Hawken: "Our minds are being

addressed by addictive media serving corporate sponsors whose purpose is to rearrange reality so that viewers forget the world around them."[9] Traditional religious values of thrift and frugality have been transposed into cults of self-indulgence. In the words of Walter Wink: "Consumerism has become the only universally available mode of participation in modern society. The work ethic has been replaced by the consumption ethic, the cathedral by the skyscraper, the hero by the billionaire, the saint by the executive, religion by ideology."[10]

Meanwhile, the media are used to create a political culture friendly to unfettered corporate power. The myths proliferate: Big government is bad; big business is good. Cut the taxes that translate the needs of the people into public policy, "so that the people themselves can decide how their money is spent." Shred the safety net that guarantees basic human rights for all people; but by all means increase tax breaks and other forms of corporate welfare. Private wealth is sacred; public wealth in the form of decent schools, a livable environment, national parks, and transportation systems drains the economy and costs jobs.

◆ Domination systems seduce, beguile, or force decent people to do beastly things. Having served a congregation that included a number of executives of multi-national corporations, I have a sense of the human pain involved when talented people are trapped in leadership positions in domination systems. Many of my parishioners were living for the first time in beautiful homes, their families enjoying a luxurious lifestyle supported by six-figure salaries. We can understand how hard it would be for these people to challenge the corporate system that was granting them such privileges. With the reward and incentive system demanding their total loyalty to the corporation, it would take great courage to risk losing it all by blowing the whistle on inhumane practices. The litany became familiar: "How long do you think I would last if I spoke my mind? Besides, if I am fired, someone with fewer scruples will move in."

◆ Domination systems assume the guise of an idolatrous religion. William Greider charges that free-market dogma has become "an enthralling religion, a self-satisfied belief system that attracts fervent and influential adherents."[11] The free-running, uncontrolled global economy is worshiped as the savior that will bring a utopian future. Futurist Hazel Henderson calls modern economists "thought police" who, far from being spokespersons for an objective science, act "more like priests defending the true faith against heretics." They ridicule social reformers who challenge their "orthodox theology" of free-market dogma. What are the values of this idolatrous religion? The idealization of greed, the inhumane exploitation of people and nature, dishonest gain, and predatory aggression make up its code of ethics.

CREATING ALTERNATIVE FUTURES

Can anything be done to intervene in a powerful system that seems to be running beyond human control? The Christian answer is *yes*. Institutions may hurt human beings, but human beings created them and maintain them—and can change them.

I have noted that domination systems contain the seeds of their own demise. As powerful as they truly are, they are also vulnerable. Free-running capitalism invariably overreaches. The mad rush to increase capacity dumps products on a market that cannot absorb them. The resulting glut in production precipitates a crisis of instability, retrenchment, or even collapse. In addition, uncontrolled corporations do their best to undercut the purchasing power of consumers who must buy their products. Through layoffs, cuts in salaries and benefits, and relocation to areas of cheap labor they shrink their own markets. Left to their own devices, corporations will even undercut government policies that secure their own future. Examples abound: In New England, where I live, the fishing boats anchor idly at the docks because overfishing has depleted stocks. The unregulated clear cutting of forests means the eventual collapse of the industry. Farming "from horizon to horizon" without soil conservation practices, or irrigating with irreplaceable fossil water threatens future agri-business profits as well as food production. Lobbying successfully for cuts in the taxes that support good roads, airports, bridges, and postal services increases the cost of doing business.

At last, when a crisis looms on the horizon, wise business leaders cry alarm and ask government to intervene to save the system. Or sectors of the economy, such as labor organizations or civic groups, mobilize to demand structural changes. Hopefully, reforms can be made before a collapse brings widespread human suffering, as we saw in the Great Depression in the U.S. or more recently in the failure of Soviet and Eastern European economies.

One of the most hopeful signs on the horizon is the development of international agreements, norms, and institutions designed to curb destructive commercial practices and protect the global human interest. Increasingly we see the importance of the United Nations and its agencies in bringing key players together to forge the instruments needed to assure the human future.

The recently released *Human Development Report 1997* illustrates the research and early warning role of the UN. Commissioned by the UN Development Programme (UNDP), the report warns of disturbing trends in the global economy and makes recommendations for the future. Unless globalization is better managed in the public interest, authors of the report demonstrate, poor countries and poor people will become increasingly marginalized. Already annual losses to developing countries from unequal access to trade, labor, and finance have been estimated at $500 billion, ten times what they receive in foreign aid. Forty-four of the poorest countries, involving more than a billion people, have been hurt by world trade provisions.

The October 1997 issue of *United Nations Digest*, a publication of the Women's Division at the UN, summarizes the recommendations of the UNDP for a system of global policies to "make markets work for people, not people for markets":

◆ *An international policy environment for poverty eradication.* Without policy management at the global level, international economic crises, such as the collapse of the Mexican peso in 1994 and the crisis in Asian financial markets in 1997, will surely emerge.

◆ *A fairer global trade system.* The products of developing countries should be on a par with those of industrialized countries. The liberalization of markets to enable poor countries to export goods, such as textiles, should be accelerated. Agricultural export dumping should be banned.

◆ *A partnership with multinational corporations to promote growth for poverty reduction.* Of the world's 100 largest economies, 50 are countries and 50 are megacorporations. An incentive system should be put in place to encourage multinational corporations to contribute to poverty reduction and to be publicly accountable and socially responsible.

◆ *Action to stop the race to the bottom.* International action is needed to stop countries from exploiting labor and offering low wages to attract foreign investment. Such institutions as the International Labor Organization, which support respect for workers' rights, should be strengthened as well as similar institutions for environmental protection.

◆ *Selective support for global technology priorities.* Global research and development have been biased toward the needs of rich countries. The poor are left with little access to information superhighways and the education and skills to drive them.

◆ *Debt relief.* The highly indebted poor countries need debt relief now. Relief—defined in terms of debt stock and debt service—to the 20 worst-affected countries would cost between $5.5 billion and $7.7 billion, less than the cost of one Stealth bomber.

◆ *Easier access to private capital.* Private capital is bypassing areas of desperate need, especially Africa. And funds delivered through bilateral and multilateral assistance are failing to fill the gap. Bilateral aid has fallen to 0.28 percent of industrialized countries' overall gross domestic product—the lowest level since aid targets were set in 1970. This trend must be reversed, and aid must focus more on poverty eradication.

AWAKENING CIVIL SOCIETY

One will observe throughout this study that solemn international agreements are seldom implemented unless the people organize to demand it. Citizen action alone is effective in translating international norms into national law and monitoring the enforcement of the announced policies. More and more courageous people are forming coalitions to stand up against corporate colonialism. They are envisioning new futures and creating realistic alternatives to the degrading forces of the global economy.

Looking at the vast power and mind-boggling complexities of the global economy, it is all too easy to fall into a mode of cynical resignation. "What can I do about all this?" is the ready refrain. Ironically, just as we allow ourselves to fall into a stupefied paralysis, we look around to see the impressive new energies bubbling up from grassroots activists. Increasingly, coalitions seeking a just peace are networking on a global basis and unifying the combined passion and expertise of many, diverse sectors of society.

No doubt the 1992 UN Conference on Environment and Development (UNCED) signaled the emergence of a new global consciousness and an awakening global civil society. It was fascinating to observe the contrast in Rio between the Global Forum and the governmental activities at the Riocentro convention hall. The government deliberations, while essential, were formal and stilted. Delegates were pressured into avoiding many of the most crucial issues (as will be observe in chapter 3). Those of us in the Global Forum participated in a chaotic and energetic dialogue. Thousands of citizens from all over the globe gathered in "tents" in a huge park, representing hundreds of citizen action groups. They confronted the critical issues directly and developed recommendations for transforming change. Indigenous peoples, in the first global gathering of its kind in human history, articulated their concerns and insisted that global authorities hear them. The forum created The People's Earth Declaration, registering the consensus of the world's people on the essential elements of a transformed society.

At first glance, people-power confronting massive corporate conglomerates seems to a David-and-Goliath contest, with Goliath holding the most powerful weapons. We need to recall, however, that David won the battle. Civil society has the capacity to redirect the life energies of masses of people. Citizen groups can analyze issues from many perspectives and draw on the best minds to propose solutions. They can organize rapidly with the flexibility to change methods of social change as situations evolve. They have many leaders acting independently; if one is silenced, others take up the struggle. They can use the same electronic communications methods corporations use. Attacks on citizen networks often expose the brutality of the "principalities and powers," giving them new visibility and drawing new organizations to the cause.

THE ROLE OF THE CHURCH

History is replete with illustrations of the vital role church groups have played in awakening civil society. We are well equipped to confront the false theology of idolatrous institutional systems. We are skilled in articulating coherent visions for new futures, guided by the accumulated wisdom of the ages. We symbolize in our very being the finest values of the human experience. We can call upon a host of committed and courageous persons of good will. Constant litanies of repentance and forgiveness keep us in touch with the sinfulness of the human condition and the wonders of God's grace. Most of all, prayer focuses our attention on the hurts of the human family, softens our attitudes of even our enemies, and empowers us both to expect and to envision new futures.

NOTES

1. *New York Times*, February 23, 1993, p. 1.
2. In Fantu Cheru, *The Silent Revolution in Africa* (Atlantic Highlands, N.J.: Zed Books, Ltd., 1989), pp. 155-56.
3. David C. Korten, *When Corporations Rule the World* (San Francisco: Kumarian Press and Bertrett-Koehler Publishers, 1995), p. 207.
4. Ibid., p. 210.
5. William Greider, *One World, Ready or Not: The Manic Logic of Global Capitalism* (New York: Simon & Schuster, 1997), p. 104.
6. Herman E. Daly and John B. Cobb, Jr., *For the Common Good* (Boston: Beacon Press, 1989).
7. Greider, *One World, Ready or Not*, p. 455.
8. Walter Wink, *Engaging the Powers* (Minneapolis: Fortress Press, 1992), p. 6.
9. Greider, *One World, Ready or Not*, p. 149.
10. Wink, *Engaging the Powers*, p. 5.
11. Greider, *One World, Ready or Not*, p. 473.

Study Guide

Questions for Reflection

In what ways does global poverty affect human rights concerns?

Is poverty a problem in the so-called Third World countries only?

How do hunger-making and war-making systems feed on one another in Africa?

How would you describe to a critic the Christian mandate for ministries among the poor?

Why is Africa singled out for a case study in global injustice?

What is "Afro-pessimism"? How should Christians respond to it?

What is meant by the "cascading effect" in ecological deterioration?

How can the Christian community resist hunger-making systems?

Suggestions for Local Church Study/Action

The dizzying scope and complexity of global economic systems may leave us feeling helpless and paralyzed to act. "Compassion fatigue" in the face of massive human need can easily tempt us to do nothing at all. Yet we have seen again and again that Christians organized with others for persistent citizen action have driven redemptive wedges into seemingly hopeless situations. We can all do something!

◆ Challenge your congregation to become active in Bread for the World, the most effective advocacy group on behalf of the hungry of the world. Respond to calls to action as they arrive. Write to Bread for the World, 1100 Wayne Avenue, Suite 1000, Silver Spring, MD 20910 (301-608-2400).

◆ Respond to Bishops' appeals in emergency situations, giving generously to the United Methodist Committee on Relief (UMCOR).

◆ Join the Fifty Years is Enough campaign and the Jubilee 2000 campaign to influence the policies of the World Bank and the International Monetary Fund. Write for information to the General Board of Church and Society, The United Methodist Church, 100 Maryland Ave. N.E., Washington, DC 20002 (202-488-5600).Write for information to the General Board of Church and Society, The United Methodist Church, 100 Maryland Ave. N.E., Washington, DC 20002 (202-488-5600).

◆ Write to the General Board of Church and Society for information on the Alliance for UN Sustainable Development programs, a network that seeks poverty reduction, food security, sustainable livelihoods, environmental protection, and equality of opportunity.

◆ Encourage your congregation to choose at least one Advance Special project to assist in small-scale development in an area of your choice. Write to the General Board of Global Ministries, 475 Riverside Dr., New York, NY 10115 (212-870-3600).

◆ Ask your congregation to become a member of the Washington Office on Africa, our eyes and ears in Washington, D.C., to affect U.S. policy toward Africa. Respond to Action Alerts as they arrive. Write to: Washington Office on Africa, 100 Maryland Ave. NE, Suite 509, Washington, D.C., 20077-0758 (202-546-7961).

◆ Find ways to work alongside victims of poverty through Volunteers in Mission, the fastest-growing mission outreach program of The United Methodist Church. Write for information to the General Board of Global Ministries, The United Methodist Church, 475 Riverside Dr., New York, NY 10115 (212-870-3600).

◆ Organize a watchdog group in your congregation to monitor the social welfare situation in your community. Find out which coalitions are doing the most effective work.

Selected Resources

Video

No Place to Call Home (sale: $29.95; rental: $15.00)—more than 50 million men, women, and children have been forced from their homes and homelands. Many are economic refugees, forced to flee in order to survive. Others are victims of civil war or are fleeing persecution or political oppression. The video is enriched by individual stories of courage in the midst of suffering. It bears witness to models of compassionate sharing. The settings are Rwanda, Bosnia, and Guatemala. A study guide is included. Order from Friendship Press Distribution Office, P.O. Box 37844, Cincinnati, OH 45222-0844 (513-948-8733). It may be rented from EcuFILM, 810 Twelfth Avenue S., Nashville, TN 37203 (1-800-251-4091 or 615-242-6277).

Studies

Uprooted: Refugees and Forced Migrants, Elizabeth G. Ferris (New York: Friendship Press, 1998)—written for the School of Missions Study, this study tells the story of the millions of suffering people who have been driven from their homes and countries by civil war, famine, economic exploitation, or political oppression. Elizabeth Ferris reveals in graphic language the plight of the ultimate victims of demonic systems.

Global Economics: Seeking a Christian Ethic, Pam Sparr (1993; write to Service Center, General Board of Global Ministries, 7820 Reading Rd., Caller #1800, Cincinnati, OH 45222-1800)—this United Methodist book with accompanying study guide is an excellent resource, clear and concise. The chapters include these themes: "Seeking God's Treasure: Christian Ethics in an Economically Unjust World"; "How the Global Economy Works"; "Economic Issues and Christian Witness Today"; "Ideas for Leading a Global Economics Mission Study."

Books

The Silent Revolution in Africa, Fantu Cheru (Atlantic Highlands, N.J.: Zed Books, Ltd., 1989)—written by a brilliant analyst from Ethiopia, now a professor at American University, this is a devastating critique of "development" programs in Africa. After working in the development establishment for a number of years, Cheru concludes, "Development is a criminal lie that does nothing for the poor." At the same time, this is a hopeful study, since African ingenuity is creating alternative economic systems that emphasize cultural identity, self-reliance, social justice, and ecological balance.

Justice, and Only Justice, Naim Stefan Ateek (Maryknoll, N.Y.: Orbis Books, 1989)—a Palestinian liberation theology, this is a superb study of justice and righteousness in the Scriptures. Writing a theology for victims of war and economic injustice, Ateek, Canon of St. George's Cathedral in Jerusalem, seeks to promote reconciliation in the Middle East.

When Corporations Rule the World, David C. Korten (San Francisco: Kumarian Press and Bertrett-Koehler Publishers, 1995)—in the words of Archbishop Desmund Tutu, "This is a 'must-read' book—a searing indictment of an unjust international economic order, not by a wild-eyed idealistic left-winger, but by a sober scion of the establishment with impeccable credentials. It left me devastated but also very hopeful. Something can be done to create a more just economic order."

Ideology in America: Challenges to Faith, Alan Geyer (Louisville: Westminster John Knox Press, 1997)—in this prophetic and inspiring call to justice, peace, and economic democracy, Geyer proposes strategies for mainline churches and ecumenical institutions as they encounter assaults from rightwing groups. At a time when government is under attack from self-serving corporate interests, Geyer details the essential functions of government in protecting human rights and assuring social justice.

One World, Ready or Not, William Greider (New York: Simon & Schuster, 1997)—the subtitle, *The Manic Logic of Global Capitalism*, gives a clue to Greider's conviction that the global economy is a juggernaut out of control. The globalizing economy ravages the environment as it creates massive human suffering. This is a monumental and brilliant analysis of the inner workings of global capitalism.

For the Common Good, Herman E. Daly and John B. Cobb, Jr. (Boston: Beacon Press, 1989)—in this brilliant critique of mainstream economics, former World Bank economist Daly and theologian Cobb show how our growth-oriented industrial economy has created environmental disaster and global poverty. This is a constructive work, recommending constructive alternatives for redirecting the economy, building community, and assuring a sustainable future.

Caught in the Crisis: Women and the U.S. Economy Today, Teresa Amott (New York: Monthly Review Press, 1993)—this book explores in clear language the impact of the Reagan/Bush era on workers in the United States. Written by an economist for those who have no special training in economics.

War Against the Poor, Jack Nelson-Pallmeyer (Maryknoll, N.Y.: Orbis Books, 1989)—the author describes his experiences living and working in Central America. He shows how the strategy of "low-intensity conflict" victimizes the poor through economic exploitation perpetuated by terrorism and propaganda.

Mortgaging Women's Lives: Feminist Critique of Structural Adjustment, Pamela Sparr (London: Zed Press, 1994)—this study contains studies on Nigeria and Ghana, offering a clear introduction to World Bank/IMF policies.

Chapter 3

Overcoming War-Making Systems: Militarism

Everyone has the right to life, liberty, and the security of person.
—*Universal Declaration of Human Rights*

Peacemaking is ultimately a spiritual issue. It is a sacred calling of Jesus.
—*In Defense of Creation*

The militarization of the world as a result of fifty years of cold war is one of the great tragedies of our time. The militarization of the poor nations of the world is a greater tragedy. Great power struggles were played out over the backs of the poor for four decades. Many poor nations spend more on the military than on development. Much of the military equipment they buy is used to wage war against their own people. The debt crisis in nation after nation is directly related to the militarization of their societies.

You cannot squeeze an ounce of rice out of a tank! Energy and resources spent on war cannot feed hungry people or provide clean water.

On Mindanao a few years ago, the director of a rural development program sponsored by the churches said with great bitterness, "If the millions of dollars Marcos spends on the military to pacify us were spent on development, he would have no need to pacify us."

The two nations that have spent the largest proportion of their national income on arms imports for several decades are Iraq and Somalia. Iraq remains today a threat to peace in a volatile part of the world. The world was forced to spend billions of dollars to drive Iraq's invading troops out of Kuwait. Somalia collapsed into chaos under roving warlords. The international community risked the lives of peacekeeping troops in a failed attempt to restore order. To avoid mass starvation, relief agencies sent tons of relief supplies to the Somalian people. These nations stand as powerful testimony to the true nature of war-making systems.

WAR-MAKING SYSTEMS AND HUMAN RIGHTS

Looking back over this bloody century, does anyone still need to be convinced that war-making systems devastate all hope for human rights? Modern wars slaughter soldiers and civilians alike. The systematic bombing of cities during World War II brutally deprived millions of innocent victims—men, women, and children—of the right to life itself. Who knew that at the time Hiroshima and Nagasaki were destroyed in a nuclear hell that virtually every city in Japan had already been destroyed by a rain of incendiary bombs? Who remembers that the fire bombing of Dresden by the allies, a city packed with tens of thousands of refugees, probably killed as many people as those who perished in Hiroshima or Nagasaki? It is small comfort that Hitler led the way into such madness with the saturation bombing of allied cities. The demonic logic of war overwhelmed all of its participants. Meanwhile, under the doctrine of Mutually Assured Destruction, appropriately labeled the MAD doctrine, the powerful nuclear nations solemnly declared their intention to commit omnicide and even biocide in the name of a vague dogma: national security.

As I have already mentioned, warfare in 1990s has been marked by mass rape, starvation as a weapon of war, genocide by machete, and widespread torture. The thin gloss of civilized humanity has been torn asunder over and over again, revealing humankind's horrible capacity for brutality.

In the aftermath of war, millions of refugees and millions more displaced persons within their own countries struggle at the thin edge of survival. For them the hope of achieving basic human rights is a distant dream. Civil rights are a mockery where combat has ended with a military dictator in power, with nothing to prevent brutalization of the people and theft of the resources they need for life. Freedom to redress any grievances or to escape arbitrary arrest, imprisonment, and torture is denied. The power of the gun rules.

Even after war has ended, tens of millions of anti-personnel land mines remain to maim and kill people as they go out to farm. In Africa, where women, with their children often in tow, do some 80 percent of farm work, the carnage is heart breaking. Meanwhile, millions of acres of fertile farmland must lie fallow, too dangerous even to enter. At the White House Conference on Africa, Senator Paul Simon challenged the Pentagon to use its technical prowess to assist poor countries to get rid of this silent curse.

The just war doctrine has been so systematically violated in this century that we must dream a greater dream, an ancient dream: a just peace for humanity. Whatever else we must do to achieve a just peace, curbing the entrenched power of militarism is a crucial first step.

CONFRONTING THE NUCLEAR CRISIS[1]

We were carrying a great wooden cross through the Nevada desert at the entrance to a nuclear test site. At each of the traditional stations of the cross, we pinned a fitting symbol on the cross to represent the suffering of Christ and the agonies of the human family. We said prayers that the earth might be spared the devastation of a nuclear holocaust.

We had gathered before dawn. We wanted to be at the site to bring our witness to the employees as they came to work. We were part of the Nevada Desert Experience. Starting small some years ago, with only the faithful Franciscan religious standing in a prayer vigil week after week, the witness has swelled to thousands. As many as 5,000 pilgrims have come at times. The United Methodists in the Western Jurisdiction have brought hundreds. Jewish groups have come, as well as Buddhists, Moslems, and Jains. Devotees of all the world's great religions have arrived to bear witness and to pray. Many Japanese delegations, some survivors of Hiroshima and Nagasaki, have traveled across the globe to bear witness to the madness of nuclearism.

It was August 6, 1995, the fiftieth anniversary of the bombing of Hiroshima and Nagasaki. We planned a major commemoration at the Nevada test site. It was a campaign to make peace with our past, to take responsibility for what we have done, and, with the help and guidance of the great spiritual traditions of the planet, to heal the earth and ourselves.

We stood with the people of the Marshall Islands, Nuroroa, Kazahkstan, Lop Nur, and Novoya Zemlya, all victims and survivors of nuclear weapons testing. We stood with the American down-winders, atomic veterans, former test site workers, and Native American peoples. All of them had, through their work and everyday lives, seen and felt the painful effects of nuclear weapons production and testing. We came together in a spirit of peace, healing, and hope to reflect on the words of Cardinal Dom Helder Camara: "This is the site of the greatest violence on earth; therefore, it should be the site of the greatest nonviolence on earth." As we approached the worship center, we carried symbols of our faith—the great faiths of the globe—and placed them among the stones that had been gathered from sites affected by nuclearism all over the world.

> *"We are survivors of the atomic bombs dropped on Hiroshima and Nagasaki in August 1945. We experienced the atrocity of the 'hell' created in the nuclear war. We had to see thousands of people dying, writhing in agony of indescribable degree. . . .*
>
> *"We are visiting this country not to denounce you. We are here to share the truth of Hiroshima and Nagasaki with you. We feel confident that hearing our stories, you will understand our desire, and work with us to set this world free of the horror of nuclear weapons."*
>
> —A *hibakusha*, survivor of Hiroshima, in *Christian Social Action* (July/August 1995)

The Nuclear Non-Proliferation Treaty

It was fitting that in 1995, the fiftieth anniversary of the first hostile use of nuclear weapons, the Review and Extension Conference of the Nuclear Non-Proliferation Treaty (NPT) would meet at the United Nations. When the treaty was signed in 1970, the non-nuclear nations had insisted that it would be reviewed every five years, and must be renewed after twenty-five years. The nations wanted to make it clear that the nuclear states must show good faith and progress toward nuclear disarmament, or the treaty would not be renewed.

It was my privilege to be a part of a United Methodist delegation of observers to the conference. For six days, April 20-26, we heard a thorough review of the current state of nuclear disarmament struggles. Vice President Gore, along with many other prominent global leaders, told us that we were meeting at a time of unusual opportunity and great risk. He reminded us that for the first time since the tragedy of Hiroshima, we could cling to a rekindled hope that nuclear disarmament is possible.

Like those who created the United Nations, we are assembled at a moment of unusual opportunity and great risk. The confrontation between the United States and the Soviet Union has ended. Our governments have moved with great speed to put behind them a relationship based on a nuclear balance of terror. That alone profoundly diminishes the risk of nuclear war in the world, but it does not eliminate that risk. Should nuclear weapons proliferate, those risks could again increase, and the opportunity we currently have to reduce the global nuclear danger will be lost.

—Vice President Al Gore, at the United Nations NPT Treaty Conference, April 1995

With the end of the cold war, the destruction of nuclear weapons proceeds cautiously and deliberately. The Start I Treaty, when completed, will see the dismantling of 9,000 warheads, and the Start II Treaty is scheduled to remove 5,000 more from the arsenals. Discussions are beginning on Start III. Current plans should see the destruction of 90 percent of the nuclear weapons by the year 2000. What a hopeful end this would be to the bloodiest century in human history!

The Non-Proliferation Treaty was renewed permanently. It has now been signed by 178 nations. It establishes a universal norm that condemns all use of nuclear weapons and requires their eventual elimination. Within the past six years, thirty additional nations have signed the treaty, and seven nations have either halted nuclear programs or rid their countries of nuclear weapons.

That is the good news. The bad news is that the nuclear threat has not ended.

Stockpiles of nuclear weapons remain, far higher than at the time of the original signing of the NPT. The explosive power of two tons of TNT for every person on earth remains in the arsenals. More than 1,500 metric tons of plutonium, the most dangerous substance on earth, is stockpiled. Israel, Pakistan, and India have not signed the treaty and continue to threaten their neighbors with their nuclear programs.

Thanks to former President Carter's initiative, North Korea has promised to halt its covert nuclear program, but Iraq and Iran continue an irrational and dangerous defiance of the world's nuclear consensus. In New York we heard Dr. Helen Caldicott say that if a small quantity of plutonium had been added to the bombs in used in terrorist attacks in New York and Oklahoma City, tens of thousands of people would have been killed over a wide area. The security of the fissile materials being taken from nuclear weapons in the former Soviet Union has been the subject of urgent international deliberations. It is disquieting to learn that on several occasions attempts have been made to smuggle plutonium out of these countries. Methods of strict accounting and controls over plutonium have yet to be fully implemented. *The world is still a dangerous place!*

The Deterrence Doctrine

The United Methodist Church Center for the United Nations has for years provided meeting rooms and logistical support for Non-Governmental Organizations (NGOs) that gather to shape decisions at the UN, across the street. This hospitality is a vital ministry, especially since the UN is turning increasingly to NGOs for guidance on critical decisions. Officials at the UN recognize that governments often do not have the expertise needed to do background research on complex issues. They are often impelled by domestic political considerations to advocate solutions to global problems that are inadequate. NGOs can bring together the most outstanding experts from across the globe to address issues of great importance. These citizen groups can speak truth to power without fear of political reprisal.

One such NGO, which met at the Church Center during the NPT negotiations, was the International Network of Engineers and Scientists Against Proliferation (INESAP). Fifty scientists and engineers from seventeen nations, including some who helped to create nuclear weapons in their countries, had met in a series of consultations for over two years. They gathered to release a document summarizing their findings. They concluded that technical means are now at hand to rid the world of nuclear weapons and the means of manufacturing them!

The only conceivable rationale for holding nuclear weapons and threatening to use them has been to deter others from using them. Deterrence based on the threat of "mutually assured destruction" (the MAD doctrine, so well named) was for years the rock-bottom rationalization for maintaining nuclear capability. A devout Christian SAC pilot was asked how he dealt with his conscience during the time he was ferrying nuclear weapons. His answer: "We knew we must never use them, but we could think of no other way to keep the Soviets from blackmailing us with their arsenals."

Over a decade ago, the Council of Bishops declared the deterrence doctrine morally bankrupt. Some observers say we were the first mainline Christian body to insist on an unqualified condemnation of the holding of nuclear weapons. The bishops wrote: "The ideology of deterrence must not receive the church's blessings, even as a temporary warrant for holding on to nuclear weapons."

At that time the Council of Bishops was accused of being hopelessly naive for believing that the world could be free from the nuclear threat. Scarcely a prominent public figure advocated total nuclear disarmament on the basis that "the genie is out of the bottle; since we cannot un-invent nuclear weapons, we must always have at least a minimum deterrent force to protect against blackmail by rogue nations or terrorists." At the Church Center for the UN, however, an international network of scientists and engineers boldly proclaimed that the deterrence doctrine is not only morally bankrupt, but that it is technically bankrupt as well. They concluded that a world free from nuclear weapons is no longer a fanciful idea. The technical means are available to drive the menace off the face of the earth.

These scientists and engineers make a convincing case. We cannot prevent nuclear proliferation so long as any nation holds nuclear weapons, tests to invent even more dangerous ones, or manufactures and stockpiles materials that can be diverted to military use. They detail the non-nuclear methods available for deterring rogue nations from manufacturing nuclear devices. They show that the technical means to detect clandestine nuclear programs are being perfected. They contend that those who believe they are secure behind a nuclear shield are themselves hopelessly naive. Even a few weapons are like a smoldering fire: "As long as there is any fire at all, a change in the wind can produce a major conflagration. So too with nuclear weapons. A change in the international climate can provoke a new and more deadly arms race, reigniting the danger of a global nuclear war."

> *The moral case for deterrence, even as an interim ethic, has been undermined by unrelenting arms escalation. It has been discredited by the invidious discrimination between nuclear-weapon states and those that have renounced nuclear rights under the 1970 Non-Proliferation Treaty. . . . The ideology of deterrence must not receive the church's blessings, even as a temporary warrant for holding on to nuclear weapons.*
>
> —In Defense of Creation

The deterrence doctrine is the only barrier to total nuclear disarmament, and it has lost all credibility. It is not just a stupid idea; it is a horrible dangerous idea! *That emperor has no clothes!*

THE PYRAMID OF VIOLENCE

During the UN NPT conference in 1995, we spent several days with a powerful new coalition of citizens' groups, the International Citizens' Assembly Against the Spread of Weapons. The group reminded us that the nuclear threat is at the apex of a vast pyramid of violence. As essential as nuclear disarmament is, it is only a part of the huge task of ridding the world of its immense weapons burden.

At the base of the pyramid of violence is the runaway proliferation of automatic weapons and handguns flooding the streets of our cities. The powerful National Rifle Association has again and again blocked legislation that might curb the domestic arms race. Even our schools are not safe. One teacher remarked recently, "When I first started teaching, my biggest problem seemed to be keeping the students from chewing gum in class. Now, I worry that they might kill themselves!" In addition, 190 paramilitary groups operating in 36 states, many of them with ties to white supremacist groups, are reportedly stockpiling weapons. Our culture has not yet found a way to prevent the glamorization of violence in films and television.

Conventional weapons are at the heart of the pyramid of violence. As early as 1970, the United States began the long journey that, in the words of President Carter, has made us the "arms merchant of the world." Under President Nixon, in the name of containing Communism, U.S. arms sales to the developing world rose from almost $1.5 billion in 1971 to almost $15 billion in 1975. Sales to Persian Gulf nations jumped by an astounding 2,500 percent during that period. Should we be

> *The case for a nuclear-weapon-free-world is no longer a fanciful idea: "It is taken seriously by strategists, military experts, even former U.S. Secretaries of State and Defense. This is because they now concede the point—which peace movements have been making for years—that nuclear weapons diminish, rather than enhance, the security of nuclear weapon states. This process, by which Cold War thinking is being eroded, will help the non-declared weapon states as well to abandon their nuclear weapon options.*
>
> —Scientists from 17 nations, in the study *Beyond the NPT: A Nuclear-Weapon-Free World*

surprised that we were forced to fight a costly war in the Persian Gulf?

At the UN NPT gathering we were startled to learn from William Hartung, author of *And Weapons for All*, that far from diminishing at the end of the cold war, conventional arms sales have escalated dramatically. By 1993, the United States was selling 72 percent of all weapons purchased by developing nations, 90 percent to undemocratic nations. Today we sell eight times the volume of weapons as our nearest competitor. Most of these sales are heavily subsidized by taxpayer funds.

During the cold war years, we did not hesitate to sell arms to military dictators all around the world. Today autocratic governments are employing those weapons to wage war against their own people or to threaten their neighbors. Ethnic groups bent on eradicating ancient enemies use them, as we have witnessed in Bosnia, Rwanda, and Burundi. Of the 50 conflicts in the world in recent years, the United States provided weapons to 45 of them. At the conclusion of the Persian Gulf War, we vowed to stop arms sales to that region. We have instead continued to pour arms into this volatile region, in competition with our own allies.

WAR-MAKING AND HUNGER-MAKING SYSTEMS

Concern for human rights impels us to reflect on the relation between war-making and hunger-making systems. Militarism is in part a result of poverty; in part, it is a cause of poverty. War-making and hunger-making systems join in a weird dance of death, energizing and feeding off one another. Militarism thrives in a pool of injustice.

Wherever there is an abyss between the luxury of the few and the misery of the many, brutal methods are created to maintain the gap. The wider the gap, the greater the brutality. Some observers, such as noted international economist Dr. Xavier Gorostiaga, are saying that we are facing a crisis so grave that it will shape the future of humanity. I heard him call this the "first truly global crisis of civilization." The revolutions in mass communication technologies and transportation have made us aware that we are one world, one human family. But the division between the rich and the poor in that family has never been so great in human history. The concentration of power—technological, financial, administrative, and especially military—is immense and growing. Moreover, the poor are waking up and demanding justice and democratic participation in the governance of their nations. It is a time of great instability and danger.

The militarization of the poor countries is a direct result of economic and cultural domination by the industrialized, consumer-addicted regimes and the wealthy minorities who do their bidding within the poor countries. The terrorism of the state against its own people—through torture, kidnapping, murder, exile—goes into action when dominant minorities can continue their exploitation by no other means. Giant terror machines are created to force enough social order to seduce foreign capital and to protect the privileged few.

So, as the cold war thaws, military-industrial complexes seek new enemies. General Maxwell Taylor is reported to have said after the Vietnam war, "As the leading 'have' power, we may expect to have to fight to protect our national valuables against the envious 'have-nots.' " Some powerful voices are declaring that the poor of the world are our new enemies. We must prepare for "low-intensity warfare" against them, they say.

It must be said clearly: The poor are not our enemy. We do have an enemy! The common enemy of humanity is militarism in the service of injustice. We often say that an attack from extraterrestrial beings would unite the entire human family in defense of the earth. But the destructive alien presence is already among us! It is the cult of militarism, now bloated to gargantuan proportions as it feeds on the goods needed for life. Its idolatrous ideology, usually called national security, penetrates our minds and subverts the best intentions of good people, making it all the more insidious.

We know now that the only security is common security for all people. The "new world order" will not emerge from the barrel of a gun. It demands a change of hearts and minds, a transformation of values. It requires a new resolve to unite persons of goodwill all over the world to drive the hostile, alien presence from the earth. The military-industrial complexes, in all their manifestations, must be starved into weak and withered shadows of their former selves!

War-making systems, designed to make the world safe for hunger-making systems, increase their deadly power. War-making systems are hunger-making systems. Militarism wastes the resources needed for development. Militarism creates refugees by the millions, most of them women and children. Millions more are internal refugees, driven from their farms and businesses, hidden from sight in the great slum belts around major cities or in barren mountain passes. Militarism crushes democratic action to redress economic exploitation; strikes are forbidden, political opposition is rewarded with torture and death; poor villagers demanding land are driven from their homes at the point of a gun. Militarism blocks indigenous peoples, the majority in Latin America, from access to education and health services that could increase their creativity and productivity.

Why Does Everybody Come?

When they call a war, why does everybody come? Mark Twain said, "Someday they will call a war, and nobody will come." When we call a war, everybody comes. Television brings it into our living rooms in living color, day after day, until we become so used to seeing images of violent death that we become immune to the real thing.

Where does the fascination with the killing power of high-tech weapons come from? Watching the "smart bombs" steer themselves down the ventilation shafts of hardened bunkers causes some strange pride and exultation to rise up inside. Our fear and disgust of war evaporates once our troops are committed. The nation "rallies 'round the flag" to support our troops. Yellow ribbons sprout on every tree, and American flags come back from the social hall to the chancel of the church, often standing higher than the cross.

It seems that a deep, powerful, even righteous rage can be successfully tapped when leaders label the Nicaraguans or the Iranians or the Iraqis the "enemy." It is a mark of a chaotic age when enemies become our friends, and our friends suddenly become our enemies at such a dizzying pace. We are ready to lay waste our substance and sacrifice our youth for the conquest if the "pseudo-species" territorial button is pushed. Perhaps the late Carl Sagan was correct when he said that we still carry the "primitive reptile brain" around in our brain stem, ready to make us vicious if our territory is threatened.

Why can this button be so easily pushed? It is beneath the level of rationality. For years we were taught that Nicaragua was a threat to our national security. A little thought revealed that the population of Nicaragua was about the same as that of Brooklyn. But Nicaragua is a rural culture with no high-tech weapons and an average annual income of $250. So we were made to believe that a poverty-stricken "Brooklyn" was a security threat to the greatest industrial and military power on earth. Why can we be so easily manipulated by the high priests of the militarism cults?

Later I will discuss patriarchy and peace. A readiness for violence, whether domestic, neighborhood, interethnic, or international, is rooted in patriarchal systems. Patriarchal cultures, in order to exist, must enforce, teach, and constantly reinforce the negative masculine qualities of domination and aggression. From earliest childhood, people are taught in millions of homes to honor aggression in men and submissiveness in women, keeping both men and women from growing into their full potential as whole human beings in creative communion.

The Militarization of Opportunity

We can see another way in which war-making systems and hunger-making systems interact. It is the *militarization of opportunity*. For many thousands of young people, the only way up and out of urban slums or rural poverty is to join the military. Who was sent to the Persian Gulf War? A huge majority of poor people, African Americans, Hispanics, and Appalachian mountain people. One pastor told me that in two Appalachian counties where he served, almost every able-bodied man was in the Persian Gulf. They had joined the reserves, not because they wanted to kill, but so that they could get health insurance and a decent income for their families.

Many young people join the military to get job training. Recently, however, the

Pentagon announced that we couldn't count on them to do our job training for us. How will young people learn the skills they need to make a contribution to society? Former Labor Secretary Robert Reich has written that one reason why the German economy is so successful is that they invest heavily in the job training of young people who are not college-bound. We have the greatest system of higher education in the world, but we abandon thousands of young people who cannot go to college, denying them jobs and all of us the fruits of a strong economy.

Now it appears that when they call a war, the young women are eager to go, too. Many complain that they have been barred from combat duty. Their careers are damaged, they say, since in the military those who get ahead are those who have been "blooded" in combat. Women must be allowed to kill, they say, so that their careers can advance. They see this as another form of sexist discrimination. Is this a development peacemakers should welcome? Or is it another patriarchal attempt to co-opt women into cults of militarism and thus to silence their peace-making voices? What happens to a culture when not only the men, but also the women are brutalized? This development will be discussed in a later chapter.

PEACEMAKING ALTERNATIVES: AN EMERGING VISION

"New occasions teach new duties." Now we are struggling to learn our new duties in a world in revolutionary transition. Should the United States be ready to send troops into every trouble spot on earth? That question is part of a larger one: Can the international community learn to use peacekeeping methods that will *not* do more harm than good? We are learning how to use economic sanctions to force justice and peace, which worked so well in South Africa, not so well in Iraq, and were tested again in Haiti and in Serbia.

International Peacekeeping Forces

The United Nations is learning how to use international forces as buffer troops to keep combatants from hurting one another. Conciliation services and conflict resolution, such as those offered by the Carter Center in Atlanta, are being increasingly utilized. At a recent TransAfrica meeting, I heard a group of African leaders make a plea for training in methods to resolve conflicts without resorting to arms. UN agencies are encouraging regional coalitions to assist neighboring nations to make peace, as the West African nations are doing in Liberia and Sierra Leone, supported by multi-million dollar grants from the United States. The leaders of several East African countries offered their services to seek a just peace in Somalia. American forces are now in Kenya, training a permanent peacekeeping force of Africans answerable to the Organization for African Unity. A faculty member of the Naval War College in Newport told me recently that the curriculum there is changing to include courses in diplomacy and conflict resolution.

International Sanctions

A strategy that is being used increasingly to bring warring parties to the peace table is UN action to bring various levels of sanctions to bear. Elsewhere in this study, I tell of hearing Salim Ahmed Salim, Secretary General of the Organization for African Unity, pay warm tribute to the citizens of the United States, including the churches, for the vigorous anti-apartheid campaign they waged against the outlaw government of South Africa. Congressional action to force economic sanctions on that government played a key role in bringing down a vicious system of legalized racism. A reluctant Congress would not have taken that action apart from the political action campaign coordinated by the TransAfrica coalition. Organized citizen action is playing an ever-expanding role in creating alternatives to military action. Economic sanctions are being used with varying degrees of success in a number of conflict situations.

Civilian-based Defense

One of the consultants to the Council of Bishops in its nuclear study was Gene Sharp of Harvard University. He has written extensively and counseled a number of governments on nonviolent means of defense through courageous citizen action. He reported that a vast, but neglected, history exists of people who have nonviolently defied foreign invaders, domestic tyrants, oppressive systems, internal usurpers, and economic masters. We could recall Gandhi's *Satyagraha* ("soul force") campaign, which gave birth to the free nation of India, or Norway's resistance during Nazi occupation to keep schools free of Fascist control. Martin Luther King, Jr., inspired the powerful civil rights movement, which transformed a nation and in which the churches played a key role. The Roman Catholic Church empowered the Solidarity movement in Poland, which brought freedom from Communist oppression. Since that time peacemakers of the world have been en-

> *In this world of seemingly relentless violence, more and more of which might have nuclear implications, all Christians and their churches are clearly called to join in exploring every possibility of nonviolent means to a just peace. We recall once more that pacifists and just-war theorists share a moral presumption against violence; they have every reason to collaborate in peace research and education and to join in developing a more inclusive approach to peacemaking.*
>
> —*In Defense of Creation*

couraged by the nonviolent citizen action that broke the old wineskins of Communist oppression in East Germany, Czechoslovakia, and Poland. The churches played a powerful and courageous role in that struggle as well. This story, long untold, should be studied intensively by church groups intent on learning effective peacemaking methods.

The Witness for Peace movement in areas of conflict in Central America deserves to be mentioned. Many people participated in actions to monitor hostilities, document atrocities, move courageous international citizens into positions to protect villages from violent attack, and to mobilize church assistance in relief and development efforts. Many knowledgeable observers are convinced that organized church action prevented a military invasion of Nicaragua by the United States and hastened the day of peace. This experience is testimony to the power to transform society of concerted ecumenical witness and action to transform society.

Yes, we have witnessed in our time the powerful action of the God who dreams of *shalom*. Courageous people all over the world, guided and empowered by the Holy Spirit, have faced domination systems and won. But it is too early to celebrate final victory. We must not forget that entrenched military bureaucracies, enriched by vast sums of the people's money, do not give up easily. President Dwight D. Eisenhower warned us years ago that military-industrial complexes take on a powerful life of their own and must be controlled by an alert citizenry. Fortunately, we now know the transforming power of organized nonviolent action!

WAR-MAKING SYSTEMS: AN INDICTMENT

Think of the bloodiest century in human history. Think of the "Big Men" of Africa, swaggering in their gaudy uniforms and using the arms the United States and other nations supply to oppress their people and steal their resources, becoming billionaires while the people go hungry. Think of the children who continue to die because their life-giving resources are being bled away. Is it too extreme to say, "We have an enemy! A common enemy of humanity is militarism. . . . The military-industrial-scientific-media complexes in all their manifestations must be starved into weak and withered shadows of their former selves"?

When these words were proposed to the Council of Bishops for inclusion in the 1992 Episcopal Address, some of the bishops were concerned that if we used such harsh words, the young men and women in the armed forces would believe we had turned their backs on them. Some said that our military families have a hard enough time making ends meet without speaking of cutting back on their support.

We need to be clear that just as The United Methodist Church has through the years supported conscientious objectors, so also it has supported those who conscientiously serve in the armed forces. Of course, we respect and honor those who have risked their lives again and again in service to their country. All of us can tell stories of individual heroism, of great personal sacrifice, of skilled mastery of incredible technologies, of acts of compassion even in the midst of the chaos of combat. But as a young woman ensign, proud of her achievement in graduating from the Naval Academy, said, "It is just too bad that it is all for killing."

In the permanent warfare society we have evolved into since World War II, it is not only those serving in the military or working in defense-related industries who are affected. All of us are caught up in the system, profiting by it or suffering because of it. As mentioned earlier, it is the nature of domination systems that decent people are trapped into doing beastly things, often mesmerized by the rhetoric with which demonic systems try to hide their true nature.

Any criticism of war-making systems opens us to the charge that we are doctrinaire pacifists, to be dismissed outright as naive, unrealistic dreamers. Few of us believe that we can instantly, unilaterally disarm in this kind of a brutalized world. If you get tangled up with a tiger, you must develop a careful strategy for turning it loose. One South African, referring to the apartheid system, said, "These people have built a wall, and they do not know how to tear it down without its falling on them"

Since dictatorships often collapse into anarchy when they attempt to democratize, a highly militarized world is by definition an unstable world. The most careful planning by the most gifted minds must be employed to negotiate verifiable steps toward disarmament, planning for the retraining of personnel and the conversion of defense industries to a peacetime status. At the same time, we must encourage bold, independent initiatives of the type that broke the nuclear stalemate and ended the cold war.

When church leaders criticize military systems, they are often rather crudely reminded that the money supporting their buildings and programs comes from salaries earned and profits gained from the defense establishment. They are right, of course. All of us are entangled in a complex web of war-making activities. Yet, we must speak truth from the belly of that beast. We must claim our freedom to condemn war and the preparations for war, and the ideology of militarism that supports them. Somebody must dream the dream, praying and struggling for a world beyond war.

We are sometimes surprised to learn that military leaders themselves agree with us. I remember a panel on nuclear disarmament, when a man walked into the church and took his place on the panel, resplendent in the uniform of a senior officer in the Marine Corps. He stood up to say, "I fought in World War II; I fought in Korea; I fought in Vietnam!" As we steeled ourselves for a spirited attack on our peace-making activities, we were amazed to see this strong man break into tears. In a tremulous voice, he cried, "There must never be another war!"

Whether we are committed pacifists or hold to the just war doctrine—whether we believe that a standing military is an important insurance policy against international criminals—we need to be free to disengage our minds from militaristic thinking to analyze clearly the intrinsic nature of war-making systems. What is our indictment?

War-Making Systems Thrive on Falsehood

It is often said that the first casualty of war is truth. We can also say that truth is in jeopardy in any society that is engulfed in preparations for war. Chinese General Sun Tzu said more than 2,000 years ago, "All warfare is based on deception."

Winston Churchill is reported to have said, "Lying finds its highest expression in wartime, when truth must be shielded by a bodyguard of lies." Unfortunately, when we spin a fabric of lies to deceive an enemy, we end up deceiving ourselves. A recent General Accounting Office assessment of the Gulf War concluded: "The smoke the Pentagon blew in Mr. Hussein's eyes wafted back to the US. Many of the stories about infallible, invisible, almost invariably accurate weapons—selectively detailed, carefully crafted tales told to the American people and the Congress—were at best 'noble lies.' "

The GAO concluded that the reports of the military and the arms makers were "overstated, misleading, inconsistent with the best available data, or unverifiable." The Pentagon's response was that the GAO report was outdated, since all of the defects in weaponry it reported have "now been fixed."

The Pentagon uses the phrase "perception control" for its "noble lies." It is nothing new. In the 1950s the Air Force warned of a "bomber gap" and a "missile gap" in order to win the budget presumably to fill those gaps. In 1961, General Eisenhower said the gaps were a "fiction" and made his solemn warning of a "military-industrial complex" that had taken on a life of its own, bereft of public accountability or even rationality. To justify continuing to spend billions of dollars on the ill-starred "Star Wars" projects, the Pentagon staged fake tests. Their purpose: To justify future weapons spending.

"Funny, they don't look like guinea pigs!" Beverly Walker used those words on a poster of her children, which she showed to a Symposium on Nuclear Radiation and the Environment. The General Board of Global Ministry sponsored the symposium in Santa Fe, New Mexico in March 1996. Beverly, a pastor's wife and a professional archivist, grew up near the Hanford Nuclear Complex. Her poster was part of a campaign to alert the public to the health crises emerging among those who were children during the years when pink clouds of radioactive smoke were released into the atmosphere from the Hanford Complex. "They lied to us!" Beverly exclaimed. "They told us it was safe!" Beverly told us of the birth defects her children had suffered and the multiple health problems she and thousands of others suffered.

We were briefed on the medical work the Houston Methodist Hospital Complex is doing with hospitals in Kazakhstan. In the Semipalatinsk region of Kazakhstan, the Soviets had exploded some 500 nuclear warheads, 300 of them in the atmosphere. More than 400,000 persons were exposed repeatedly to radiation released into the atmosphere or seeping into the ground water. The people were told there was no danger. The medical consequences of the fallout have been horrendous. All forms of cancer proliferate in the region and stillbirths, retardation, and other birth defects are of epidemic proportions.

Both in the United States and the former Soviet Union, governments lied to the people. The cardinal right of informed consent required in all medical experimentation was deliberately violated. In 1945 alone Hanford, Washington, officials released 550,000 curies of radiation, often deliberately for research purposes. Beverly Walker said the pink smoke rising from the stacks fascinated the children. It turned the snow pink; the children played in it and made ice cream from it. In the remarkable film *Downwind of Morality,* Beverly says, "They didn't have a right to do that to me. That's my belief. And it should never happen again. Don't make me a guinea pig! Don't make my children and grandchildren guinea pigs!"

What happens when government systematically lies to its people? Cynicism and alienation tear the fabric of democracy. Many decent people drop out of the political process altogether. They leave the field under the control of highly disciplined, one-issue coalitions or ideologues of extreme persuasion. Civility becomes a casualty to strident, destructive rhetoric. It is not just the governments that lose credibility; corporations that manipulate public opinion for their own greed cause a loss of confidence in all large corporate systems. Hate groups begin to proliferate. As we saw in Eastern Europe and the Philippines, the people may rise up *en masse* and declare a lying government illegitimate.

War-Making Systems Fatten on Greed

The Congressional Budget Resolution of 1997 provided an extravagant $266 billion for defense, some $12 billion more than the Pentagon requested. As children, Americans were taught that we are unique among great nations. Our military is under the strict control of the civilian branch of government, we were told. For years now we have seen a reversal of this principle. Defense contractors and others who profit from military systems pressure Congress to manufacture weapons systems, even over the objections of Pentagon strategists. For instance, the Salt II Treaty for a nuclear weapons role back was strongly supported by the Joint Chiefs of Staff, but opposed by the President and the Secretary of State.

Again and again local commercial interests have supported unwise military procurements. For many, the military is seen as a jobs program. Deliberately distributing subcontracts for the production of strategic weapons systems into a range of congressional districts, the Pentagon garners political support. Large donations to the re-election campaigns of members of Congress from arms manufacturers are clearly a conflict of interest.

Today the Pentagon, with its political and corporate supporters, contends that we should continue wartime spending for the military so that we can "modernize our forces in order to retain technological dominance in weaponry." The credibility of that claim vanished with the demise of the Soviet Union. The Pentagon insists that we must be ready to fight two major wars at the same time, with no help from our allies. Who are these enemies? What happened to the allies who have supported us in every major war in this century? Admiral Eugene Carroll of the Center for Defense Information says, "Now it appears that America is engaged in an arms war with itself!"

Whatever happened to the Peace Dividend? Why are we spending so much on the military when we are trying to balance the federal budget and reduce huge deficits, while at the same time insisting that we can no longer support the safety net for the poor? At a peace rally at the Center for Advanced Studies in Princeton in August 1997, I heard Carroll say: "The not-too-hidden agenda of many members of Congress is delivering federal spending to their districts, and there are few better ways to do that than fattening the Pentagon budget and ordering expensive new weapons systems. The cold war provided political cover for this wasteful practice, but it is now indefensible."

War-Making Systems Turn on Their Masters

War-making systems are like Frankenstein's monster: Once unleashed, they run an unpredictable course. Jesus said, "Those who live by the sword will die by the sword." Often, sad to say, they die by their own sword. This is the boomerang effect, so often discussed.

Against the Soviets, for instance, we armed and trained the Mujahedin in Afghanistan. Now the weapons we provided are being used to destabilize the Punjab in India. The explosives we provided and the explosives experts we trained are in the control of terrorists, many of whom see the United States as the enemy. As of this writing, Kabul has been overrun by a rebel group using arms left over from the East/West struggle. Now a million people who long enjoyed one of the most liberal ways of life of any Muslim community in Central Asia are under the rule of a fanatical faction. A repressive code of conduct is being ruthlessly enforced. Women's rights are now a fiction; women are no longer allowed to hold jobs; they are covered from head to toe with the *chedori* when venturing out. Even the most ardent supporters of our involvement in the Afghan war can hardly believe this was our dream for the Afghani people.

Long ago, President Eisenhower said, "It is a question how far we can go in defending ourselves from without, without destroying ourselves from within." For centuries, war-making elites have devised ways to protect their own societies from brutalization as a result of their military adventures. As we ponder the gun fetish on television, the unbridled power of the National Rifle Association, the growth of illegal militia, the violence on urban streets and in the homes of America, is it not clear that in brutalizing others we have brutalized ourselves?

War-Making Systems War Against the Earth

The venerable watchdog of the planet's life-giving systems, the Worldwatch Institute concluded that the world's armed forces are the single largest polluters on earth. Modern warfare devastates vast areas. We need only look at the effects of defoliation in Vietnam or remember the burning oil wells in Kuwait to confirm the Institute's judgment. Or we might ponder the horrifying lingering effect of 100,000,000 land mines left over from conflicts in Africa and Asia to concede the point. The cost in malnutrition and even starvation in areas where thousands of acres cannot be farmed adds insult to the grave injury of thousands of men, women, and children who have lost limbs or life.

Moreover, the production, testing, and maintenance of conventional, chemical, biological, and nuclear weapons generate enormous quantities of toxic and radio-active substances that contaminate soil, air, and water. Vast areas in Eastern Europe are wastelands, with water and soil so polluted that they cannot support human life.

According to the Worldwatch Institute, the military use of aluminum, copper, platinum, and other non-renewable resources exceeds the entire Third World demand for these metals. The United States military burns enough fossil fuel each year to run all of the U.S. mass transit systems for fourteen years! This is a sobering thought, since the Institute predicts that within the lifetime of young people today, fossil fuel costs will rise beyond the purchasing power of even the wealthier nations.

Clearly we must make hard choices—and make them now. The biosphere cannot sustain forever our overheated, highly militarized, industrial economies. We often say that war is bad for children and other living things. War-making systems are also bad for the life-giving forces of creation on planet Earth.

SOME SIGNS OF HOPE

Lest we despair of ever seeing the dismantling of vast and powerful military systems, we should take heart at some recent developments. A rising tide of organized concern for militarism is achieving startling results. All over the world, global public opinion informed by research findings from some of the greatest minds of the century is emerging as a powerful force to transform political realities.

The recent ratification of the Chemical Weapons Treaty by the United States Senate signals hope for the elimination of weapons of mass destruction. The banning of biological weapons is an important milestone. The most dangerous and seemingly intractable problem is the struggle for nuclear disarmament. Even here important breakthroughs are being achieved:

The World Court Decision

On July 8, 1996, the World Court declared the threat to use or the actual use of nuclear weapons a violation of international law. This was an unprecedented, historic moment, a giant step toward peace through international law. Despite strong appeals from four of the five nuclear powers to back away from the issue, the International Court of Justice, the highest judicial body in the world, unanimously concluded: "There exists an obligation to pursue in good faith and bring to a conclusion negotiations leading to nuclear disarmament in all its aspects under strict and effective international control."

The World Court qualified its opinion, unfortunately. Under extreme circumstances of self-defense, in which the very survival of a state would be at stake, the court said it could not definitely conclude whether the threat or use of nuclear weapons would be lawful or unlawful. Officials of the United States immediately used that loophole to claim that the court favored the status quo on nuclear deterrence. Officials of a number of other nations immediately condemned that gratuitous interpretation.

We who live with the hope that people power organized to demand change can transform society should take heart. It was a coalition of non-governmental organizations that launched the World Court Project in 1992. They were able finally to persuade the World Health Assembly, and then the UN General assembly, to ask the World Court for a ruling.

While the advisory opinion of the court is not legally binding, it expresses the clear consensus of the highest legal authority on earth. Citizen groups around the world, and especially those in the nuclear states, can challenge their governments to review their nuclear defense policies. The onus is now on governments to prove that they are moving with dispatch toward compliance with the many international demands for nuclear disarmament, including Article VI of the Nuclear Non-Proliferation Treaty.

The Comprehensive Nuclear Test Ban Treaty

On September 10, 1996, by a vote of 158 nations in favor, three opposed, and five abstaining, the UN General Assembly adopted the text of a comprehensive nuclear test-ban treaty. India, Bhutan, and Libya cast negative votes; the abstainers were Cuba, Lebanon, Mauritius, Syria, and Tanzania. The heart of the treaty is in the first sentence of Article I: "Each state party undertakes not to carry out any nuclear weapon test explosion or any other explosion, and to prohibit and prevent any such nuclear explosion at any place under its jurisdiction or control."

This effectively puts an end to a period of more than four decades that saw at least 2,000 nuclear explosions in the atmosphere, underwater, and underground. Thus we dare to hope that all of the surviving downwinders, "guinea pigs" for national security dogma, will be able to rest easier. They may take heart that others will not have to suffer as they have suffered.

The treaty is flawed in that it bans only nuclear explosions, but not all nuclear tests. The hope that no nation would have to live in fear that another will achieve strategic advantage with a technological breakthrough is thus qualified. The United States Department of Energy plans to spend billions of dollars to build an elaborate system of sophisticated laboratory facilities. These will enable it to maintain, test, modify, and design another generation of nuclear weapons well into the next century. Other nations might view with skepticism the solemn protestations that the United States has no plans to resume production of nuclear weapons. Nuclear weapon science will be advanced through computer simulations, laboratory experiments, and "zero yield" underground tests. Large non-nuclear explosions will be conducted, along with miniature contained thermonuclear explosions. The data from these experiments will be run through the world's fastest supercomputers.

What is the purpose of this expensive program? Why should billions of dollars be spent on a weapons system that the international community has solemnly pledged to destroy? The program is rationalized as a way to ensure the safety and reliability of the nuclear weapons stockpile "for the foreseeable future." Non-nuclear nations that voted to extend the NPT Treaty indefinitely must question the sincerity of the United States in agreeing "to pursue negotiations in good faith on effective measures relating to cessation of the nuclear arms race at an early date and to nuclear disarmament."

Nevertheless, the Comprehensive Test Ban Treaty is an important achievement. It makes more difficult technological breakthroughs that could allow the creation of even more diabolical weapons. This is a giant step toward easing the fears that fueled the arms race.

Ambassador Richard Butler, who sponsored the draft resolution in the UN General Assembly, declared that the treaty would stand as "the unique expression by the world community of a norm of behavior." Morally and politically, and hopefully one day a legal standard thoroughly entrenched in international law, it binds nations to put the nuclear era behind them. Ambassador Butler continued: "As every day passes and that norm is observed, then it becomes harder and harder politically in international relations, and even in domestic politics, for a government to take the decision to break that norm."

France discovered the power of world public opinion when it cynically resumed nuclear testing in the Pacific immediately after the passage of the NPT Treaty. Spontaneous boycotts of French products in international markets soon pinched the pocketbooks of the French people. Clearly a culture of peace is emerging and exerting its power.

The Canberra Commission

> The first requirement is for the five nuclear weapon states to commit themselves unequivocally to the elimination of nuclear weapons and agree to start work immediately on the practical steps and negotiations required for its achievement.

This straightforward declaration is the heart of the report to the UN General Assembly from the Canberra Commission on the Elimination of Nuclear Weapons. Created by the Australian government as an independent commission in 1995, its mandate was to propose practical steps toward a nuclear-free world. At the same time it was charged to recommend ways to maintain stability and security during the time of transition and beyond.

Reporting to the UN General Assembly on September 30, 1996, the commission called the current situation "highly discriminatory and thus unstable," which "cannot be sustained." To continue to tolerate nuclear weapons in the hands of a few states while the entire world is threatened is to court disaster.

Some of the immediate steps the report recommends is to remove the warheads from delivery vehicles, end the deployment of non-strategic weapons, reduce drastically the size of U.S. and Russian arsenals, and make a universal pledge of no-first-use. The commission elected not to set out a precise timeframe for the elimination of all nuclear weapons, but urged the setting of guidelines that "would drive the process inexorably toward the ultimate objective of final elimination."

The commission issued a warning to those who would relax their peacemaking efforts on the assumption that the danger has passed: "It is false to claim that the world has traversed successfully the most dangerous phase of the nuclear era and is now on the path to modest, passively deployed nuclear forces that will deliver the asserted benefits of deterrence at much reduced risk—the so-called 'low-salience' nuclear world."

The commission reminds us that even if Salt II is fully implemented, Russia and the United States will still have a nuclear arsenal of around 7,000 operational warheads, plus others in reserve. In the words of Jonathan Schell, we dare not "drowse our way to the end of the world."

A quick glance at some of the distinguished members of this commission convinces us that they deserve to be heard: Robert McNamara, former U.S. Secretary of Defense and President of the World Bank; General Lee Butler, former Commander in Chief of the U.S. Strategic Air Command and the U.S. Strategic Command; the late Jacques-Yves Cousteau, leading campaigner for world survival issues; Professor Joseph Rotblat, winner of the 1995 Nobel Peace Prize, who worked on the atom bomb in Liverpool and Los Alamos, now President of the Pugwash Conference on Science and World Affairs; and Dr. Maj Britt Theorin, member of the European Parliament and President of the International Peace Bureau and Parliamentarians for Global Action.

Military Leaders on the Elimination of Nuclear Weapons

One of the most gratifying events took place on December 5, 1996. Two distinguished United States military leaders issued a statement calling for the abolition of nuclear weapons. They are General Lee Butler, former Commander-in-Chief of the Strategic Air Command and of the U.S. Strategic Command, who was in charge of all Air Force and Navy nuclear weapons and an architect of our nuclear policy; and General Andrew Goodpaster, Supreme Allied Commander in Europe from 1969 to 1974. Theirs were joined the next day by a similar statement signed by sixty military leaders around the world. The joint statement was carefully nuanced:

As senior military officers, we have given close attention over many years to the role of nuclear weapons as well as the risks they involve. With the end of the Cold War, these weapons are of sharply reduced utility, and there is much now to be gained by substantially reducing their numbers and lowering their alert status, meanwhile exploring the feasibility of their ultimate complete elimination.

> *We believe the time for action is now, for the alternative of inaction could well carry a high price. For the task that lies ahead, there is need for initiatives by all who share our conviction as to the importance of this goal. Steady pursuit of a policy of cooperative, phased reductions with serious commitments to seek the elimination of all nuclear weapons is a path to a world free of nuclear dangers.*
>
> —Joint Statement from 60 Senior Military Officers.

The officers reminded us that great risks remain in continuing to hold nuclear weapons: accidents and unauthorized launches; seizures or thefts of weapons or the means to make them and their possible use by terrorists; proliferation to other nations. With each passing day, these threats increase.

The officers recommended the rapid reduction of nuclear arsenals step by step to "the lowest verifiable levels consistent with stable security." If existing weapons were removed from alert status and the warheads placed in guarded storage, confidence to take the next steps would be enhanced. The ultimate objective is clear: *The complete elimination of nuclear weapons from all nations.*

The Campaign to Ban Landmines

Few successes in the long struggle for disarmament illustrate the power of citizen action more dramatically than the signing of a treaty to ban land mines. On October 10, 1997, it was announced that Jody Williams, coordinator of the International Campaign to Ban Land Mines, was co-winner, along with the campaign, of the Nobel Peace Prize. Williams began working for the Vietnam Veterans of America Foundation in 1991. Today 1,000 NGOs in more than 60 countries are advocating to rid the world of these horrible weapons, which kill or maim 26,000 people a year, some 80 percent of them civilians. Their dream came to fruition with the signing of a treaty for a total ban on anti-personnel land mines. More than 90 nations had signed the treaty as of this writing. Russia had announced its intention to sign. Some believed that the death of Princess Diana, the most visible supporter of the campaign, encouraged the Nobel committee to give priority to the cause. We can be sure that the persistent witness of hundreds of thousands of citizens organized into thousands of coalitions assured the victory. We can be grateful that the churches, once again, played a key role. Jody Williams paid tribute to Church World Service and the wider community when she said, "Congratulations to you for being a part of this amazing effort. Your contribution has been critical at so many junctures."

Jody Williams was on target when she said, "This is what humanity is calling out for." She was also persuasive as she said, "But now we need governments like the United States, Russian, India, and Pakistan to come on board." Many were distressed that the United States refused to join this overwhelming expression of the conscience of humanity.

The International Criminal Court

In June of 1998 a diplomatic conference in Rome is scheduled to adopt a treaty establishing an International Criminal Court (ICC). Shortly after the UN was formed, a commission was mandated to codify the Nuremberg principles. Progress on the initiative was mostly paralyzed during the cold war years. A newly assigned ad hoc committee reported in 1995 that while most countries favored establishing a permanent court, several major nations remained opposed or undecided, including China, France, the United Kingdom, and the United States.

In 1995 a group of non-governmental organizations met in New York to form the NGO Coalition for an International Criminal Court. Since then the coalition has been actively seeking the support of a wide range of civil-society organizations, including human rights, international law, judicial, humanitarian, religious, peace, women's, and parliamentarians. With pressure from the coalition and the majority of countries, the UN General Assembly asked that a preparatory committee be established. The PrepCom met twice in 1996 to discuss issues such as the court's jurisdiction, the definition of crimes, the role of the Security Council, trigger mechanisms, general principles of criminal law, and the cooperation between the court and national jurisdiction. At long last it begins to seem possible that a permanent court to try war criminals will be established. Peace through international law, a dream of the ages, may come to fruition in our time.

OUR BIBLICAL MANDATE

A little more than a decade ago the Council of Bishops declared the deterrence doctrine morally and spiritually bankrupt. Now we hear learned scientists declare it technologically bankrupt and senior military officers term it militarily bankrupt. Surely we live in a time of hope! The church bells of the world should be ringing in celebration. The architects of peace should be honored with ticker-tape parades through the streets of the cities. National holidays should be declared to celebrate our emerging liberation from decades of dread. No doubt it is too early for a final celebration—but every step along the way so tortuously gained should surely be the occasion for prayers of praise and thanksgiving. Reflection on the Scriptures reveals our special vocation to work for peace, to celebrate peace, to pray for peace.

> *Now, therefore, we ask you, our sisters and brothers, to join with us in a new covenant of peacemaking. . . . We ask you all to open again your hearts, as we open our hearts, to receive God's gracious gift of peace; to become with us evangelists of* shalom, *making the ways of Jesus the model of discipleship, embracing all neighbors near and far, all friends and enemies, and becoming defenders of God's good creation; and to pray without ceasing for peace in our time.*
>
> —from the Pastoral Letter, "In Defense of Creation"

The Old Testament

Many words in the Old Testament speak of peace. None is so rich as *shalom*. *Shalom* is more than the absence of war. It is positive peace, a just peace: harmony, wholeness, health, and well-being among human beings and with creation itself. It is harmony among all the creatures in God's good creation. The will of God, the yearning of God, the power of God for the earth family is *shalom*. The entire earth is promised the joy of *shalom*:

90

For you shall go out in joy,
    and be led back in peace;
the mountains and the hills before you
    shall burst into song,
    and all the trees of the field shall clap their hands.
Instead of the thorn shall come up the cypress;
    instead of the brier shall come up the myrtle;
and it shall be to the LORD for a memorial,
    for an everlasting sign that shall not be cut off.
(Isa. 55:12-13)

The Hebrew Bible speaks of covenant, the "covenant of peace," which binds the people to God. In the covenant of *shalom*, justice and peace, peace and security, love and justice are all one (Jer. 29:7). When "the Spirit is poured upon us from on high," we will dwell in a just peace:

Then justice will dwell in the wilderness,
    and righteousness abide in the fruitful field.
The effect of righteousness will be peace,
    and the result of righteousness,
        quietness and trust forever.
My people will abide in a peaceful habitation,
    in secure dwellings, and in quiet resting places.
(Isa. 32:16-18)

The testimony of the ancient word is clear. No true security can be found without peace, and no peace without justice. When nations rule unjustly and depend on military might for their security, they reap devastation:

You have plowed wickedness,
    you have reaped injustice,
    you have eaten the fruit of lies.
Because you have trusted in your power
    and in the multitude of your warriors,
therefore the tumult of war shall
        rise against your people,
    and all your fortresses shall be destroyed.
(Hos. 10:13-14)

The New Testament

The Hebrew Bible forecasts the coming of One who will be the Prince of peace. Jesus Christ came, heralded by angels who sang: "Glory to God in the highest, and on earth peace!" He bestows the most special blessings on peacemakers. He commands us to love our enemies. The Sermon on the Mount summarizes his teachings:

> "You have heard that it was said, 'An eye for an eye and a tooth for a tooth.' But I say to you, Do not resist an evildoer. But if anyone strikes you on the right cheek, turn the other also; and if anyone wants to sue you and take your coat, give your cloak as well; and if anyone forces you to go one mile, go also the second mile. Give to everyone who begs from you, and do not refuse anyone who wants to borrow from you. You have heard that it was said, 'You shall love your neighbor and hate your enemy.' But I say to you, Love your enemies and pray for those who persecute you, so that you may be children of your Father in heaven; for he makes his sun rise on the evil and on the good, and sends rain on the righteous and on the unrighteous." (Matt. 5:38-45)

The apostle Paul's letters announce that Jesus Christ is "our peace." Christ has broken down the "dividing wall of hostility," creating one humanity and overcoming all enmity:

> For he is our peace; in his flesh he has made both groups [Jews and Gentiles] into one and has broken down the dividing wall, that is, the hostility between us. He has abolished the law with its commandments and ordinances, that he might create in himself one new humanity, in place of the two, thus making peace. . . . So he came and proclaimed peace to you who were far off and peace to those who were near. (Eph. 2:14-17)

It is Christ who calls us to ministries of reconciliation and equips us for those ministries. We become ambassadors for a new reign of God, a new order of love and justice:

> So if anyone is in Christ, there is a new creation; everything old has passed away; see, everything has become new! All this is from God, who reconciled us to himself through Christ, and has given us the ministry of reconciliation; that is, in Christ God was reconciling the world to himself, not counting their trespasses against them, and entrusting the message of reconciliation to us. So we are ambassadors for Christ, since God is making his appeal through us; we entreat you on behalf of Christ, be reconciled to God. (2 Cor. 5:17-20)

NOTE

1. Parts of this section first appeared in *Christian Social Action* (July/August 1995).

Study Guide

Questions for Reflection

In what ways do war-making systems threaten basic human rights?

What is the impact on civil and political rights of military institutions?

Is the just-war doctrine still useful after its systematic violation over the past decades?

What realistic alternatives to military methods are available for building and keeping the peace?

In your opinion, is the total abolition of nuclear weapons feasible in our time?

How do you see yourself as a follower of the Prince of peace?

Do you see signs of hope for peace in the events of the past decade?

Suggestions for Local Church Study/Action

◆ Become a part of the Peace With Justice Network of The United Methodist Church. Contact the Peace With Justice Program, General Board of Church and Society, 100 Maryland Ave., N.E., Washington, D.C. 20002 (202-488-5600).

◆ Observe Peace With Justice Week. Write to the Office for World Community, Room 670, 475 Riverside Drive, New York, NY 10115 (212-870-2424; fax 212-870-2055).

◆ Join the U.S. Campaign to Ban Landmines. Write to the Vietnam Veterans of America Foundation, 2001 S St., NW, Suite 740, Washington, D.C. 20009 (202-483-9222; fax: 202-483-9312).

◆ Become a part of the Abolition 2,000 campaign. This campaign is an international citizens' network with an 11-point program calling for governmental action on such issues as nuclear test ban, no first-use commitments, nuclear weapons-free zones, and advocating for a global decision by the turn of the century to abolish all nuclear weapons. Call the General Board of Church and Society, Washington, D.C., for information (202-488-5600).

◆ Keep informed of the activities of the Coalition for an International Criminal Court. Write to WFM, 777 UN Plaza, 12th floor, New York, NY 10017 (fax: 212-599-1332).

◆ Become a part of the World Council of Churches' Programme to Overcome Violence. As a part of the effort, a two-year "Peace to the City" campaign will culminate at the Eighth Assembly in December 1998. The WCC is building "jubilee communities"—communities of justice, peace, and ecological sustainability—at local, national, and international levels. To receive information on the campaign, send an e-mail to majordomo@info. wcc-coe.org. Include subscribe pov-l (without quotes) in the body of the letter.

◆ Advocate for legislation to curb the traffic in conventional weapons. One example is the Code of Conduct on Arms Sales Act, first introduced by Representative Cynthia McKinney and Senator Mark Hatfield and still pending in Congress. The act would forbid sales of weapons to any non-democratic regime. Plan to stay in contact with the Arms Transfer Working Group, Friends Committee, 245 2nd St. NE, Washington, D.C. 20002-5795 (202-547-6000; fax: 202-547-6019).

Selected Resources

Video
Landmines: Overcoming a Lethal Legacy—a 9:09 minute-long portrayal of the critical issue that tens of millions of land mines are killing and maiming men, women, and

children is available through Church World Service. To rent, call 800-297-1516 (fax: 219-262-0966).

Books

The Idea of Disarmament, Alan Geyer, rev. ed. (Elgin, Ill.: Brethren Press, 1995)—this is one of the most detailed analyses of the struggles for disarmament, written by one of the most gifted Christian peacemakers of our time.

And Weapons for All, William D. Hartung (New York: Harper Perennial, 1994)—a recent analysis of how the United States has become the arms merchant to the world. It shows the way America's multiumillion-dollar arms trade warps our foreign policy and subverts democracy at home.

In Defense of Creation: The Nuclear Crisis and a Just Peace (Nashville: Graded Press, 1986)—this Council of Bishops' study of the nuclear crisis was hailed as one of the most influential documents of its time on nuclear issues and the most unequivocal condemnation of the deterrence doctrine by a mainstream Christian body. It has been translated into six languages and studied in the former East Germany, Western Europe, the former Soviet Union, Korea, and Japan.

"Women Peacing Worlds Together," ed. Susan Perz, *Journal of Sacred Feminine Wisdom* (1996). Order from Passion Flower Creations, Inc., P.O. Box 9, Claremont, CA 91711 (909-626-2333).

State of the World, Annual Worldwatch Institute report on Progress Toward a Sustainable Society (New York: W.W. Norton, annual)—the Worldwatch Institute is the leading research center measuring the vital signs of the health of the earth. The annual reports are translated into 27 languages and used by the public, by environmental activists, by national governments, by UN agencies, and by the development community. Write to the Worldwatch Institute, 1776 Massachusetts Ave., NW, Washington, D.C., 20036 (202-452-1999; fax 202-296-7365; email wwpub@worldwatch.org.

A Will for Peace, Herman Will (Washington, D.C.: General Board of Church and Society of The United Methodist Church, 1984)—Will, a long-time peace activist and "Mr. Peace" in The United Methodist Church for 37 years, traces the history of peace making in the denomination for the past few decades.

Chapter 4

Challenging Desert-Making Systems: Destruction of the Environment

"The right to a safe environment must be included in an updated charter of human rights."

—Pope John Paul II, New Year's Day 1990

Peacemaking in the nuclear age, under the sovereignty of God, requires the defense of creation itself against possible assaults that may be rationalized in the name of "national defense."

—*In Defense of Creation*

One of my early memories as a boy growing up on a large Iowa farm was discussion of soil conservation. I recall the county agent speaking at a meeting in our Methodist church. As he entered the pulpit, he carried a glass of water with him. I supposed he planned to drink from it, but I hoped he would not, for it seemed rather polluted. As he concluded his speech, he raised the glass on high. I noted that the bottom third of the glass contained soil that had settled. Pointing to it, he said, "Friends, I dipped this water from your local river on my way here. You will note the soil at the bottom. This is your topsoil. It is on the way to the Gulf of Mexico. When it is gone, how will your children live?" It is distressing to think that over these past decades, not only is the soil still eroding, but also waters and air are increasingly polluted. Global warming and holes in the ozone layer are totally new concerns.

It was the great orator and Squamish Chief Seattle who over a hundred years ago warned us of the long-term consequences of ecological carelessness. The version of his speech that has become a favorite of so many was actually enhanced by a radio announcer just a few years ago. But a pastor in the New York Conference, the late Mark Anderson, a member of the Mohawk people, gave me a copy of the original text. Chief Seattle dictated a letter to the Great Chief in Washington, D.C., as the United States government was trying to buy his people's ancestral lands:

This earth is precious to God and to harm the earth is to heap contempt on its creator. The Whites too shall pass, perhaps sooner than all other tribes. Continue to contaminate your bed, and you will one night suffocate in your own waste.

If we sell you our land, love it as we've loved it. Care for it as we've cared for it.

Hold in your mind the memory of the land as it is when you take it . . . and with all your strength, with all your mind, with all your heart, preserve it for your children, and love it . . . as God loves us all.

Chief Seattle, observing the arrogant attitude of the oncoming whites, the careless waste of natural resources, the senseless killing of animals, concluded with the warning: "Your appetite will destroy the earth, and leave behind only a desert!" This becomes our metaphor for the ecological wantonness so characteristic of our time. Indigenous peoples who have lived in deserts for centuries remind us that deserts are beautiful places, containing plants for food and medicine. Where water can be found, many desert areas are fertile and remarkably productive. But turning green and fertile lands into deserts through human greed and arrogance is an insult to the Creator.

Upon our retirement, my wife, Gwen, was asked to become director of spiritual formation at the Scarritt-Bennett Center in Nashville. Maxine Beach, then Director of the Center, said to me, "Since you used to be an Iowa farmer, if you will create our Urban Demonstration Garden and composting project, you may come with Gwen." I promptly bought a tiller and dug up part of the campus. The sign in front of the garden now reads "In Defense of Creation," a tribute to the nuclear study by the same name, led by the Council of Bishops. The garden demonstrates how an urban institution can compost its grass clippings, leaves, kitchen waste, and other organic matter and turn it into vegetables, herbs, fruits, and flowers. At the same time it creates a quiet and beautiful meditation center. Its presence testifies to the commitment of the Women's Division and the Church at large to preserve and restore nature. A garden is a "gentle conspiracy" to challenge the millions of acres of grass surrounding urban institutions. The American lawn uses more commercial fertilizer than India and China combined, while causing more pollution of rivers and ponds than all the surrounding farms, according to Bill Mollison of Permaculture.

In Nashville, other urban institutions would send delegations to consider such a garden on their grounds. One day a group of young people came with their counselor. They were residents of a group home for youth rescued from violent families. As we discussed the philosophy of the garden, I quoted a Native American, Ed McGaa (or Eagle Man), who in a moving address said that if Chief Seattle were to return today, "his heart would fill with tears" to see what we have done to his native land. He would grieve at the great hole in the sky we have created, the acid rain that kills fish and trees, the global warming that threatens coastlands and fertile plains, the toxins released into the air and water, the clouds over Chernobyl. Eagle Man cried, "What does it take to wake up world governments to the global environmental threat? Can we not see that *the miner's canary is dying*—that we must save the earth if we are to save ourselves?"

The young people visiting the Nashville garden had not heard of the miner's canary. I explained that in an earlier time, methane gas would seep into coal mines. Completely odorless, it would kill without warning. The miners learned to bring a caged canary into the mines. They watched it closely for any sign of trouble. If the canary fell from its perch, they scrambled out of the mine in a hurry. "What is the miner's canary today?" I asked the youth. One young man said, "I have heard that the frogs around the world are dying. Maybe they are warning us that something is wrong."

The young man was right. The skin of frogs and other amphibians is so sensitive that they are unusually vulnerable to environmental threats. Many scientists now believe that the thinning of the ozone layer is exposing them to too much ultraviolet radiation. Now we learn that frogs in Minnesota are being born with horrible birth defects. No one is yet sure of the cause. Remembering those magical spring evenings when the frogs would begin to sing, it was illuminating to read in a newspaper about E. B. White, writing from his saltwater farm in Maine. So much is clouding our future these days, he said, "Yet I know . . . that on some not too distant night, somewhere in pond or ditch or low place, a frog will awake, raise his voice in praise, and be joined by others. I will feel a whole lot better when I hear the frogs." But suppose that on one warm spring evening the frogs no longer sing. Could this be our miner's canary?

THE BEST OF TIMES AND THE WORST OF TIMES

So much is being written about the environment these days that it is not easy to sort it all out. At times we could to be overwhelmed with despair at the monumental scope of the problem, feeling powerless to do anything about it. Therefore, we need to take heart at the signs of the world's awakening. We know the situation is grim, but powerful new coalitions are mobilizing to stop the mayhem and undo the damage.

The respected Worldwatch Institute, since 1974 one of the most credible sources of knowledge on progress toward a sustainable society, keeps its finger on the pulse beat of the globe. Its annual report to the world is the *State of the World*, now published in 27 languages and studied by governments, UN agencies, environmental activists, and others around the world. Some 500 professors in U.S. col-

> *Some . . . have implied that . . . we need not worry overmuch about pollution or carbon dioxide or whatever—that the world is a self-cleaning oven. They ignore the point that we might be the baked-on crud.*
>
> —Bill McKibben,
> *The End of Nature*

leges and universities use it as a textbook. Since ours is the best of times and the worst of times, the publication each year contains enough bad news to alert us to the need for urgent action and enough good news to energize us to faithful response. Let us reflect on some observations from *State of the World 1997*. First, the bad news:

The Worst of Times

◆ Since the nations of the world signed the Convention on Climate Change at the Earth Summit in Brazil in 1992, most scientists agree that the threat of global warming is growing rapidly. Carbon dioxide in the atmosphere is at its highest level in 150,000 years—and escalating alarmingly. The factories and automobiles of the industrial nations continue to spew greenhouse gases into the atmosphere at record levels. At the same time, the rain forests, which can cleanse the air of carbon products, are being systematically destroyed. The earth is heating up so rapidly that the resulting climate change will be unpredictable and disruptive. As global temperatures rise, floods, droughts, fires, and local heat waves will increase. Sea levels will rise within a few decades, inundating coastlines and submerging Pacific islands.

◆ Since the Earth Summit, the government of the United States has failed to ratify the Convention on Biodiversity or the Law of the Sea. It has failed to meet targeted goals on greenhouse gas emissions. It has cut back on its funding for UN environmental agencies.

◆ World population has grown in this century from 1.6 billion to the 6 billion projected by the year 2000. Since the Earth Summit in 1992, world population has expanded by 450,000,000 people, equal to the combined populations of the United States and Russia. With 88,000,000 new mouths to feed each year, many nations are threatened with ecological and social disaster within a few decades.

◆ Food production is falling behind demand. The reserve stocks in the world's grain bins have fallen to fifty days of consumption, the lowest recorded level. The millions of new mouths to feed each year are straining the earth's capacity to meet their needs. In addition, Asian economies have been growing rapidly, where half of the world's people live. With rising affluence, Asians are eating more meat and eggs and drinking more beer, all of which use much more grain for each calorie of food produced.

◆ The share of food production that depends on the unsustainable use of water and land is increasing. In the United States, production on 21 percent of irrigated land depends on water being pumped from deep pools of fossil water deposited by ancient ice melts. That water will never be replenished. Oceanic fish stocks are no longer growing, and in some places are falling disastrously. Global warming threatens to harm food production by creating more droughts, floods, and destructive storms. With rapid urbanization, fertile lands around the world, which could feed millions of people, are being paved over.

◆ The use of chlorofluorocarbons (CFCs) has created a hole in the ozone layer as large as the U.S. They are used in aerosol spray cans, refrigerators, air conditioners, and a number of manufacturing processes. The latest research shows that 95 percent of the ozone layer is lost over Antarctica, and losses over northern population centers are two to three times worse than predicted. Loss of the ozone layer exposes all living things to harmful ultraviolet light. Skin cancer rates among humans have already escalated. Sensitive species such as frogs are dying. The long-term effects on all plants and animals are unknown. Even after harmful chemicals are no longer released into the atmosphere, it will take decades before the ozone layer can regenerate itself.

◆ Environmental specialists now recognize tobacco smoke as an especially virulent form of air pollution. Smoking kills millions of people every year. In 1995, Oxford University scientists reported that tobacco use brought premature death to three million people. The developing nations, where cigarette smoking is growing dramatically, accounted for one million of those deaths. If current trends continue, tobacco will kill ten million people annually by the year 2025. The World Bank estimates that within thirty years tobacco will kill more people than AIDS, tuberculosis, and childbirth complications combined. Meanwhile, the U.S. government continues to subsidize tobacco farmers and the promotion of tobacco sales in the developing nations.

◆ As noted in chapter 2, economists distort the true picture and give a false sense of progress by measuring economic growth in terms of Gross Domestic Product (GDP). This method of accounting fails to distinguish between economic transactions that add to quality of life, community health, and natural habitat and those transactions that destroy them. Worse, economists portray this destruction as economic gain.

The Best of Times

◆ The largest gathering of heads of state in human history came together in Rio de Janiero in 1992, along with some 40,000 representatives from citizens' groups, in the UN Conference on Environment and Development, or Earth Summit. Agenda 21, a 40-chapter plan of action, was adopted. It contained agreements on goals such as protecting wetlands and deserts, reducing air and water pollution, improving energy and agriculture technologies, managing toxic chemicals and nuclear waste, and reducing disease and malnutrition.

◆ Since Rio, the UN Commission on Sustainable Development, charged with implementing the plan, has met annually to craft specific programs to put the international consensus into action.

◆ More than 117 governments have formed commissions to prepare national sustainable development strategies, as required under Agenda 21. While the results are uneven to date, the machinery for future global cooperation is emerging. Governments have signed a number of agreements, including guidelines for safety in biotechnology, the protection of fish that swim across the boundaries of national waters a new Desertification Convention, stronger measures to ban the export of hazardous waste to developing countries, and the protection of oceanic environments from land-based pollutants.

◆ New coalitions of leaders in business and industry are entering the environmental struggle. Insurance companies, agribusiness firms, the banking community, and others worry about the future health of their investments if the environment deteriorates. An example is the World Business Council for Sustainable Development and the sixty insurance companies that gathered in Geneva in 1996 to urge reductions in greenhouse gases.

◆ The powerful World Bank has embraced the challenge of sustainable development. It has strengthened its environmental impact standards and withdrawn support from some destructive projects, such as the Arum Dam in Nepal.

◆ The International Conference on Population and Development in Cairo in 1994 established the links among population growth, social inequity, material consumption, and environmental degradation. A new coalition of women's and human rights groups shaped a plan of action to slow population growth. They agreed that population growth can be controlled only through empowering women, reducing poverty, and meeting urgent social needs for education, health care, and economic opportunity.

◆ More than thirty-one countries have stabilized their populations, slowing world population growth. India, China, Indonesia, and Brazil have achieved dramatic drops in average fertility. Stringent control measures in China, such as the one-child-per-family law, have cut China's fertility rate from six births per woman to 1.9 births in less than thirty years, slightly below replacement level. Long criticized for its coercive methods, the program is slowly being softened to a more humanitarian approach.

◆ In response to the ozone crisis, the international community has mobilized with unprecedented speed. World leaders met in 1987 to adopt the Montreal Protocol. It was signed immediately by 24 nations and the European Community, and it has been ratified by 150 countries. Strengthened further in London in 1990, the protocol requires a full phase out of CFCs and other destructive chemicals by the year 2000. The results have been dramatic. Within seven years, production of CFCs dropped by 76 percent! Scientists and policy makers worked with industry leaders in a historic example of global cooperation. Chemical companies began immediately to develop substitutes for harmful chemicals. Manufacturing processes were transformed radically across a range of industries. For instance, those responsible for a range of cleansing processes in manufacturing discovered that CFCs were not necessary—plain old water would do. Countries like China, seeing that their refrigerators would not sell if they used CFCs as coolants, quickly moved to develop ozone-friendly units.

In less than a decade, we have witnessed the capacity of the international community to reverse the dangerous course of ecological tragedy. Citizens have organized around the world to demand change. Powerful financial and political leaders are getting the message that the human imprint on the earth has grown so large that life-sustaining systems are in danger. The stern warning of the Worldwatch Institute is being heard: "We are conducting a massive and somewhat reckless experiment, the consequences of which are difficult to predict."

Success in curbing further danger to the ozone layer shows what the human family can accomplish. Industry leaders learned that they can adapt quickly to environmental crises that threaten their future, along with the future viability of the biosphere. They could achieve it even while thriving economically. The old fears that environmental action will lead to loss of jobs or the ability to compete in world markets have proved false. Meanwhile, industry and developing nations have learned to work together in new ways, through a number of cooperating UN agencies. Millions of people—scientists, diplomats, NGO activists, business leaders, and governmental officials—are now working tirelessly to make the impossible possible. We have run out of excuses. Humanity is developing the tools to overcome the remaining critical problems in the "global commons."

It is important to note that little happens to curb the power of domination systems until aroused citizens organize into effective coalitions to demand action. Just as it is true that "the price of freedom is eternal vigilance," so it is equally true that freedom from the ravages of rogue institutions and their allies requires passionate, persistent, effective citizen action. Never say that individuals cannot make a difference. Only individuals of faint heart and attitudes of indifference or despair fail to contribute to the social and spiritual transformations the times demand. And those who insist on working alone are weakened from the start.

HUMAN RIGHTS AND EARTH CARE

What are some of the relationships between human rights and earth care? The UN *Declaration* does not mention environmental rights. With the escalating scope of the ecological crisis becoming more urgent, human rights to a productive and sustainable environment must be guaranteed in public policy. In the words of Pope John Paul II, spoken on New Year's Day 1990: "The right to a safe environment must be included in an updated charter of human rights."

The growing edge of human rights struggles today involves the concern for environmental justice. Clearly, people will be able to enjoy basic human rights only if they are allowed equitable access to adequate nutrition, clothing, and shelter. This means that the ecosystems that provide the means of survival must be protected and enhanced. Therefore, all persons have a right to protection from harmful pollutants of air and water. All persons have a right to clean water, productive agriculture, equitable food distribution, and access to the biosystems that sustain meaningful work. All persons have a right to far-sighted government policies that assure the long-term sustainability of the means to life. It is difficult to see how any human right can be protected for long without a healthy environment.

We were reminded at the WCC conference on Justice, Peace, and the Integrity of Creation in Seoul that the struggle for justice and earth care is two sides of the same coin. To say that we are so committed to justice ministries that we have no energy left for environmental activities is to miss an important dimension of the justice struggle: To work for justice is to work for the integrity of creation; to work for creation demands the struggle for justice. When human rights are violated, the earth suffers. When the earth suffers, basic human rights cannot be achieved, and economic and political rights are compromised.

Justice is *offended* and the earth wounded by a global economy that condemns the vast majority of the earth's people to poverty. This hunger-making system is a desert-making system. It forces the poor of the earth onto marginal lands where they must overgraze the grass, denude the forests, and destroy the topsoil in order to survive. Poverty and ecological degradation feed off each other in a descending spiral of devastation.

Justice is *outraged*, and the earth suffers from environmental racism, which inflicts polluting industries and hazardous waste dumps on poor neighborhoods where people of color and indigenous peoples predominate. Pollution continues because the poor have no power and the powerful don't care.

Justice is *abused* and the earth damaged by those who cut down rain forests for the profits of the few, forcing out indigenous peoples who have lived off the forests and cared for them for generations. With the loss of the forests, the climate is altered in destructive ways; manmade drought over large sections of sub-Saharan Africa and terrible floods in Bangladesh illustrate the problem.

Justice is *defiled* and the earth despoiled by environmental sexism, which in the name of development bars millions of women from access to the fields and forests they have carefully tended for generations, while ignoring their productive wisdom and forcing them to cannibalize their environment. One woman in Guatamala spoke for the dispossessed women of the earth when she said, "We are consuming our future in order to feed our children."

THE INTERNATIONAL PEOPLES' TRIBUNAL ON HUMAN RIGHTS AND THE ENVIRONMENT

A brief summation of the stories of people whose rights are being abused in the environmental struggle should convince us that earth care is a human rights issue. In June 1997, the first meeting of the International Peoples' Tribunal on Human Rights and the Environment gathered at the UN. Twelve cases were heard from among the thousands of situations where individuals and groups are suffering environmental and human rights abuses. Such cases are destined to increase as environmental degradation escalates.

Among those who spoke was Wangari Maathai from Kenya. I first met her at the White House Conference on Africa in 1994, where she made an impassioned plea for justice and sustainable development for her people. This courageous woman founded the Green Belt Movement in Kenya by planting seven trees in her backyard. The grassroots organization that grew from her efforts mobilizes women and children to restore the forests. Thanks to the thousands of volunteers she has inspired, more than 15 million trees have been planted in Kenya, producing income for more than 80,000 people! The movement has been expanded to over 30 countries in Africa. The effort is critical, because over half of Africa's forests have been felled in the twentieth century alone. Most of the people of these countries depend on wood for fuel. When fuel is scarce, people suffer from malnutrition, overcultivated fields create erosion, and land cover loss creates barren wastelands. As a result of her ef-

> *The Green Belt Movement is a bottom-up approach to development. It has no blue print, preferring to rely on a trial and error method using the expertise, knowledge and the capability of the local people. It addresses both the symptoms and the causes of environmental degradation. It adapts what seems to work and quickly drops what doesn't. It prioritizes on meeting the felt needs of communities: creating jobs, improving the economic status of women, transferring farming techniques and tools, providing wood-fuel for rural populations and the urban poor, fighting malnutrition especially by planting fruit trees and indigenous food crops, protecting forests. . . . While addressing these and other environmental issues the Green Belt Movement also identifies and works on economic and social issues which are likely to have a negative impact on the environment.*
>
> —Wangari Maathai at the White House Conference on Africa

forts to oppose destructive development schemes, Maathai has been repeatedly jailed and beaten.

Speaking at the International Peoples' Tribunal on behalf of the Women's Caucus, Wangari Maathai condemned the world's power blocs that put profits before people. She detailed a twelve-point action plan on "What Women Want for the Earth": gender equality, elimination of poverty, guided globalization to ensure fair, just trade and corporate accountability; preservation and equitable sharing of resources; access to clean drinking water; safe, clean energy; sustainable production and consumption; education and training; and recognition that women's rights are human rights. She cried, "Why can we not agree on an earth charter similar to the UN *Declaration of Human Rights?* Why can't we realize that we have only one earth, that we are all in it together? No one will be safe until all of us are safe."

At the Earth Summit, two legally binding instruments were signed. The first, the Climate Control treaty aimed at reducing the production of carbon dioxide through decreasing the use of fossil fuels. The second, the Biodiversity Convention was meant to protect the knowledge and lifestyles of indigenous communities that depend on biodiversity. Those who came to testify at the International Peoples' Tribunal highlight the failure of governments at all levels to fulfill these obligations. Among those who presented claims to justice were these:

◆ The Gwich'in (People of the Caribou) of Alaska are disturbed by the development of oil by international companies on the critical calving grounds of the caribou. Disturbance of the calving process endangers the future of the herds upon which the Gwich'in people depend for their livelihood.
◆ The people of the Sovereign Dineh Nation (Navajo) in Black Mesa, Arizona, are being evicted to implement mining activities by the Peabody Western Coal Company. Corporate arrogance has created pollution, environmental degradation, and the unsustainable overuse of a pristine aquifer.
◆ The National Youth Council of the Ogoni People in Nigeria testified to the "economic terrorism" of Royal Dutch Shell. Forced evictions following the illegal appropriation of Ogoni lands, pollution by petrochemicals and dumping of refinery wastes, are among the abuses that have devastated the life of the people. Any attempt to demand justice has been met with deadly force.
◆ Burmese Farmers of the Tenasserim region testified to the oppression of the Myanmar Oil and Gas Enterprise in league with the Burmese military regime. Campaigns of violence, intimidation, forced labor; the forcing of women and girls into sexual slavery; and confiscation of property have created refugees as the people have fled for their lives.
◆ The Mexican Citizens of Tabasco suffer from severe ecological degradation caused by exploitation of the petroleum reserves by PEMEX, Mexico's national

oil company. Police action has forced people off their lands. Floods, salination of lakes, contamination of drinking water, and poisoning of the food chain result from the arrogant disregard for people and the land.

◆ Recherches Internationale testified on behalf of the people in the Essequibo Riverian Area of Guyana. Gold mining activities by North American multinational corporations are polluting the waters of the area. Rupture of a tailing dam released cyanide into the river that sustains the livelihood of some 23,000 people.

◆ The International Coalition for Justice in Bhopal, India, warned that the release of poisonous gases, which blanketed a vast area, killing many people while they slept, could be repeated in other regions. Union Carbide ignored warnings of a safety audit at their Bhopal plant in an arrogant disregard for human rights and the environment.

◆ The Garifuna Grassroots Movement (New Dawn) from Honduras described the effects of a government program of tourist development. Land loss and evictions, degradation of resources, and environmental destruction have led to the marginalization of the people and the resulting poverty.

◆ The International Campaign for Tibet testified to the impact of unsustainable development by the Chinese occupying forces. Serious environmental degradation has gone hand in hand with human rights violations, as Tibetans have been impoverished by the loss of their lands.

TOWARD A WORKING THEOLOGY OF EARTH CARE

Whatever our position in life, the range of our resources, or the limitations of our energy, we can all do something meaningful about earth care. We can recycle. We can shop wisely, supporting those companies that practice sound environmental policies. We can grow an organic garden, composting readily available materials, or form a coalition to organize a growers' market in the neighborhood. We can join environmental groups that advocate for public policies that protect the earth and human rights groups that seek environmental justice. We can study and pray and teach. If ideas are in short supply, we can keep the pamphlet *101 Ways to Save the Earth* handy. Every last person can make a contribution.

Far more important, we can seek the mind of Christ on these issues. We can become clear about our working theology of creation. As we clarify our own theological convictions, we can seek ways to implement them, and we can witness to them.

As bishop of New York, a few years ago I was asked to co-sponsor a consultation between religious and environmental leaders. Senior executives of major environmental groups and the UN Environmental Programme (UNEP) met with religious leaders. Representatives of environmental groups made a strong appeal: "We need the churches! Environmental groups cannot provide the philosophical and spiritual motivation which will support people on a path of environmental concern over the long, hard journey ahead." They were asking us to do what we do best: to clarify and teach basic values informed by modern realities and rooted deeply in the traditions and scriptural heritage of our faith.

I am indebted to Wesley Granberg-Michaelson, staff member of the World Council of Churches, for suggesting that in practice we all subscribe to one of three working theologies: a theology of domination, a theology of stewardship, a theology of relationship.

A Theology of Domination

In the words of Granberg-Michaelson: "This assumes that humanity's God-given duty is to exploit the Earth in meeting any needs and fulfilling any desires. Any form of technology—regardless of its environmental recklessness—is sanctioned in this task; Gen. 1:26-28 is the proof-text often quoted."[1] The command to "subdue" the earth and to "have dominion" over the earth is taken out of context and distorted to justify exploitation and greed.

The word *duty* in this discussion is interesting. We have evolved a society in which it has become not only our right but also our duty to exploit the resources of the earth for human gain. We have developed an economy that rewards corporate leaders for making decisions that damage the earth. In a strange twist of irony, it has become the duty of lumber company executives to cut every last tree if necessary to maintain jobs and corporate profits. It is now the duty of the mining company executive to extract minerals in a way that will maximize profits for the shareholders. It is the duty of the stockbroker to inform her or his clients to sell stocks in a company if its profits begin to slip as it retools to stop polluting air or water. It is the duty of military officers to prepare for war and to conduct war, even though vast areas of the earth are despoiled and nuclear winter remains a horrible possibility. It is the duty of every corporate executive to declare the environmental costs of production as "externals" and to force the community to bear the costs of clean up. It is the duty of a parent to provide the "good life" for the family as defined by current levels of consumption, even though scientists continue to warn us that the world cannot sustain such a drain upon its resources.

What turns economic institutions into desert-making systems? They are made up of a vast network of institutions, regulations, and practices based on an arrogant will to subdue, to conquer, to use up or pollute natural systems. They are prime examples of domination systems. In the words of John McPhee, they include "any struggle against natural forces—heroic or venal, rash or ill-advised—when human beings conscript themselves to fight against the earth, to take what is not given, to rout the destroying enemy, to surround the base of Mt. Olympus demanding and expecting the surrender of the gods."[2]

Who can forget the disastrous floods along the Mississippi River? They inundated and despoiled millions of acres of prime fertile farmland and hundreds of towns. Soon afterward a friend sent me a newspaper clipping that charged that patriarchal attitudes and assumptions fueled the destructive power of the river. For decades the U.S. Army Corps of Engineers had worked to "tame the river." In the words of one spokesman for the Corps, justifying the vast system of locks, dams, and barriers built to prevent the Mississippi from taking its natural course, "This nation has a large and powerful adversary. . . . We are fighting Mother Nature. . . . It's a battle we have to fight day by day, year by year; the health of our economy depends on victory."[3]

The militaristic language of conquest reveals the reigning spirit not only of the Corps, but also of a nation built on a will to conquer a continent. It is no accident that the wanton destruction of 80,000,000 bison on the prairies was mainly a scorched-earth military policy to starve out the Plains Indians. Native Americans were aghast as they observed the rotting carcasses of bison as far as the eye could see—"one great slaughter-house," as one observer termed it. Native Americans thought the pioneers demon possessed to rape natural resources with such blind ferocity.

One of the most illuminating challenges to a system of environmental domination is *Cadillac Desert*, by Marc Reisner, the subject a PBS television series by the same name. The book has been compared with Rachel Carson's *Silent Spring* in its social impact. Studying the federal water development history of the United States, Reisner terms it "creative vandalism," a "vandalization of both our natural heritage and our economic future."[4] While in the short run it has brought impressive agricultural and economic gains and made possible the settling of great cities like Los

> *It is not my contention that chemical insecticides must never be used. I do contend that we have put poisonous and biologically potent chemicals into the hands of persons largely or wholly ignorant of their potentials for harm. We have subjected enormous numbers of people to contact these poisons, without their consent and often without their knowledge. If the Bill of Rights contains no guarantee that a citizen shall be secure against lethal poisons distributed either by private individuals or by public officials, it is surely only because our forefathers, despite their considerable wisdom and foresight, could conceive of no such problem.*
>
> —Rachel Carson,
> *Silent Spring*

Angeles and Phoenix, it has done so at great expense to natural resources. In the end it contains the seeds of its own destruction. Rivers have dried up, most of the wetlands that supported flocks of migrating birds have dried up, the great salmon runs are dead or dying. The history, beauty, and diversity of river valleys has been lost, along with great oak and cypress swamps. The Corps of Engineers brags that it has converted 26 million acres of marshy or flood-threatened land into cropland. Apparently they do not care that wetlands prevent floods, offer protection for newborn fish, and are a habitat for migrating birds.

Reisner reminds us that we cannot ultimately win in a struggle against nature. We can only hope to work with natural forces to assure our survival. Millions of acres of irrigated lands are now poisoned with salt. Tons of silt are building up behind dams. Aquifers have been thoughtlessly mined. Rivers have reclaimed flood plains again and again, and dams have collapsed to devastate vast areas downstream and kill thousands of people. Reisner asks who is going to pay to restore wetlands and wild rivers and lakes and beautiful valleys, "now that more and more people are discovering that life is impoverished without them?"[5] Thinking of the loss of innumerable species of birds, fish, and animals, we are reminded of the warning of Chief Seattle that we shall all die of a "great loneliness" when the other creatures of the earth are gone.

It is not that the development of water resources is undesirable. The point is that the militaristic attitudes of the Corps of Engineers and the Bureau of Reclamation, along with their supporters in Congress, have blinded them to the awareness that their objectives could have been met with far less destructive methods and technologies. A type of idolatry, an "industrial-technological fundamentalism" possessed them. In the Christian community, we know a better way.

A Theology of Stewardship

As described by Granberg-Michaelson, "this stresses humanity's obligation to be a wise caretaker of the Earth. Instead of subduing the Earth, from Gen. 1:28, we are asked to 'tend the garden,' from Gen. 2:15. The emphasis is on using resources wisely, remembering they are not our own but only entrusted to us for care." The dominant scriptural image defining the role on earth of Adam, whose name means "earth creature," is to till and keep the garden of life: "The LORD took the man and put him in the garden of Eden to till and keep it." To till the garden is to work it, to serve its inherent needs. It connotes respect, indeed, reverence and even worship. To keep the garden is to watch over it, to preserve it. Both actions focus, not on the expected utility of the garden for human beings, but on the needs of creation. To till and keep the garden is to serve the Creator by caring for creation. The early commands to subdue or to rule over creation are softened by a clear description of the spirit and style of human mastery over the land and other creatures. The Hebrew Scriptures give to humanity the special status of ruling over the rest of creation. To use that status to exploit, endanger, pollute, and destroy has no justification in Scripture.

According to the creation story, Adam, the protohuman, was called to be a gardener. It may require an act of faith for people in urban centers to think of themselves as gardeners. A clergyman who grew up in Brooklyn illustrates the point: "Where I grew up, milk came in bottles and cartons. When they told me where it really comes from, I thought that was the most bizarre thing I had ever heard. I refused to drink milk for years!" As a highly urbanized people, we need to find intentional ways to recall that we are creatures of the earth. As Native American spirituality expresses it, we do not weave the web of life; we are a tiny strand in the web of life.

In the Social Principles of The United Methodist Church, the stewardship doctrine is expressed:

All creation is the Lord's, and we are responsible for the ways in which we use and abuse it. Water, air, soil, minerals, energy resources, plants, animal life, and space are to be valued and conserved because they are God's creation and not solely because they are useful to human beings. Therefore, we repent of our devastation of the physical and nonhuman world. Further, we recognize the responsibility of the church toward lifestyle and systemic changes in society that will promote a more ecologically just world and a better quality of life for all creation.[6]

A sense of the stewardship of the earth roots deeply in our biblical faith. To be faithful to the Creator who graciously gives us life, we work to overcome dominating, exploitative institutions and practices.

Yet a theology of stewardship is limited. Applied to the biosphere as a whole, it can be dangerous. For many people, stewardship implies a managerial relationship to the whole of nature. Our task in this view is to govern and order nature wisely, as a benevolent monarch. Like the "spaceship earth" image, it implies that humanity is in the control room, guiding and directing creation. In reality, as some biologists now say, the biosphere is similar to a living organism. It is self-regulating and self-correcting in unbelievably complex and mysterious ways.

For instance, physicist Brian Swimme reminds us that for a billion years the earth has regulated the oxygen content of the atmosphere in the range of 21 percent, overcoming massive disturbances like asteroid impacts and volcanic eruptions. Too little oxygen, and organic life dies. Too much oxygen, and a lightning bolt could ignite the forests of the earth. The assumption that human beings can micromanage ecosystems is already courting disaster. To be a good steward of the earth is to vow not to damage its powerful, yet fragile, forces of evolution and renewal. In addition, we will energetically support those activities and policies that promise to repair the damage already done by human arrogance and greed.

We dare not forget the challenge to our arrogance recorded in the book of Job. God asks Job: "Where were you when I laid the foundation of the earth? Tell me, if you have understanding. Who determined its measurements—surely you know!" (Job 38:4-5). No, we do not know. We can never know. It is dangerous to pretend that we are ultimately in charge around here.

A Theology of Relationship

Even deeper than a theology of stewardship is a theology of relationship, or "kinship," as Native American peoples often describe it. The earth is our mother; other creatures are our brothers and sisters. For us, the creation has value and beauty not only because it has utility for human beings, but also because God sustains and dwells in it. We are strands in a complex web of existence that is infused with the grace of God. Our first privilege is to trust, enjoy, and cooperate with nature, not to try to dominate and exploit it.

One of the greatest gifts to humanity from the Bible is the revelation that within God's creation we can discover order, wisdom, and trustworthiness that manifest God's presence and grace (see Genesis 9). God has covenanted with the earth; God's faithfulness upholds the world; through "seed time and harvest, cold and heat, summer and winter," God's steadfast love assures the dependable order of all the earth systems. The refrain "the steadfast love of God" reverberates throughout the psalms.

In the Sermon on the Mount, the essence of Christian ethics, Jesus specifically invites us to be liberated from the anxiety of those who do not trust God to care for them. He says:

> "Therefore I tell you, do not worry about your life, what you will eat or what you will drink, or about your body, what you will wear. Is not life more than food, and the body more than clothing? Look at the birds of the air; they neither sow nor reap nor gather into barns, and yet your heavenly Father feeds them." (Matt. 6:25-26)

Even when hardly aware of it, we rely every day on the faith that the ecological systems that sustain us are safe and stable. The seasons of the year, leaving and returning as surely as life itself, remind us that the steadfast love of God is revealed in their ebb and flow.

A CONSERVATIVE THEOLOGY OF EARTH CARE

Let us reflect even more deeply on a faith sufficient for an ecological age. Remember the challenge of senior executives of the major environmental organizations at the New York consultation: "We need the churches!" They confessed that they are not equipped to offer the theological underpinnings of faithful ecological action, nor do they have direct access into local communities that the thousands of congregations offer: "More outlets than the post office."

Fundamentalist Christians, as represented by some TV evangelists, have long charged that the environmental movement is a Communist plot to befuddle the minds of our youth. Since Communists are now hard to find, the charge is that the environmental movement is "new age" theology and thus heretical. Some theologians argue that the veneration of nature is pantheism or nature worship, a practice that is foreign to the Scriptures. For that reason, it may be instructive to reflect on the most orthodox of Christian doctrines, the doctrine of the Trinity. Does it support ecological activism?

That question is doubly important, since some observers have charged that the Christian tradition itself is a major cause of our current ecological crisis. Christians are being blamed for the crisis! Lynn White, an American historian, is the most prominent of these critics. His argument is quoted again and again in environmental publications. He writes that Westerners feel "superior to nature, contemptuous of it, and willing to use it for our slightest whim." What is the source of this attitude? It is "the Christian axiom that nature has no reason for existence but to serve man." This "Christian arrogance" toward nature must be overcome if we are to solve our environmental problems.

We might rush to deny our moral culpability. We might protest that Judeo-Christian cultures have no monopoly on ecological sin. Indeed, almost every civilization has abused its environment to some degree if its technologies allow it. The jungle-covered ruins of great Mayan cities and recurrent famines through the ages testify that overuse of natural resources, runaway population growth, and war have laid waste to vast ecosystems, often with catastrophic results.

The opening of former Communist countries to the world's gaze has revealed that a zealous anti-Christian regime is capable of ecological mayhem. Is it not ironic? The horrible ecological devastation in the former Soviet Union came after the Communists had won a vicious power struggle against the Russian Orthodox Church, the most ecologically aware branch of Christendom. Russian President Boris Yeltsin declared, "We have inherited an ecological disaster!" Every major river is polluted, one-fourth of the drinking water is unsafe, and 35 million people live in cities whose the air is dangerous to breathe. Vast areas of Central Europe are disaster zones. Millions of acres of land can grow nothing. Sickness and death among infants and children have reached epidemic proportions in industrial areas of the Czech and Slovak peoples.

Yes, it is easy to protest that Christians alone are hardly responsible for the rape of the earth. That having been said, we must listen to voices of concern from within the Jewish and Christian communities. They encourage us to confess that our doctrine and practice have indeed played an important role in Western culture's ecological negligence and abuse.

For instance, Father Thomas Berry, former Roman Catholic priest Matthew Fox, and others from within the Roman Catholic tradition charge that the churches have focused so narrowly on issues of sin and salvation and the divine-human relationship that they have neglected the creation motif in Scripture. A Neo-Platonic dualism invaded the church with Augustine, separating body and soul, material and spiritual, nature and humanity, secular and sacred, even women and men. The latter is always seen as superior and the proper domain of faith.

We must confess that billions of Christians throughout the ages, both in their interpretation of Scripture and in their daily practice, are implicated in ecological sin. We do not have to agree that Christianity alone is to blame in order to agree that we need ecological reform in Christendom!

Are we on solid ground scripturally and historically to re-envision the Christian faith to be earth friendly? Can an ecological ethic be built on Christian foundations? It is essential to look again at the biblical record in the light of the emerging ecological crisis. We do not need to espouse a radical new faith or a romanticized Native American spirituality or new age thinking to be environmental activists, although valuable wisdom can be gleaned from these and other sources. A vital ecological motif runs from Genesis to Revelation. The strain continues through the creation mystics of the Middle Ages, on through the Protestant Reformers, and to contemporary theology and practice.

The Trinity and Earth Care

Surely nothing is more sacred or richer in Christian tradition than the doctrine of the Trinity. Christians from an early time have taught that the one true God is known through three persons. God is revealed through the creation. God is revealed through Jesus Christ. God is known intimately through the indwelling Holy Spirit. Can this doctrine be the bedrock upon which an ecological spirituality and ethic can be built?

We Believe in God, Maker of Heaven and Earth

All of the classical creeds begin with a confession of faith in God as the maker of heaven and earth. In the beginning, God—in the beginning, God created—God created the heavens and the earth and all that is within them—God created Adam (earth creature) and Eve in God's own image—God looked upon all that God had made and declared it very good. The creation story establishes that God is the owner of the earth and its occupants: "The earth is the LORD's and all that is in it, the world and all who live in it" (Ps. 24:1). The first commandment to the earth creature is to till and keep the garden of life (Gen. 2:15). To till and keep the garden of life, we have observed, is not to own or exploit it, but to care for it and preserve it for future generations and its rightful owner, the divine Creator.

Yahweh, the God of Israel, not only creates, but also is faithful to the covenant made both with the people and with the Creation (Gen. 8:22; 9:9-10). Psalm 104 portrays the Creator as intimately involved in the sustenance of the natural order. The lions "seek their food from God." The covenant with Noah and his descendents includes a promise that never again will the dependable creation be subject to arbitrary destruction. The "steadfast love of God" of which the psalmists sang would continue to push back the chaos out of which order was created (Gen. 1:3-8).

Several strains within theology today take the doctrine of creation very seriously, seeking to integrate it with modern scientific knowledge. On the Protestant side, process theology is influential and intellectually satisfying.

Process theology develops an evolutionary and organic view of creation. God is seen as a "lure" that pervades the universe. Creativity is universal throughout the cosmos. The divine reality interpenetrates every moment of existence. It is God who dreams new possibilities. God blesses the world with unrealized opportunities, opening up space for freedom and self-realization. This divine power acts through enticement and persuasion, but is the most effective power in reality. Every being as it emerges partakes in the powerful vision of God.

Process theologians teach that God is active in the world, working to overcome evil and to sustain, restore, and enhance creation. The *shalom* vision of the Scriptures is not just the dream of God for the world; the power of God is active in bringing into being peace, justice, and harmony among all the creatures of the world. When we work for justice, peace, and the integrity of creation, we are working in harmony with God and we know God. Activity to save the earth is not guided by commandments from above, but through creative encounter with the heart and soul of creation, the creating God.

From within the Roman Catholic community, the creation spirituality of former priest Matthew Fox is influential. He believes that the ethical values of earth care emerge from a "living cosmology." By this he means a new creation story now being formed by the union of biblical insights, the teachings of the medieval creation mystics, and scientific understandings of the evolution of the universe.

Fox and other theologians from that tradition, such as Theilhard de Chardin and Father Thomas Berry, seek to overcome the division between the holy and the world. Separating the creation from the Creator is the "great disaster" of human history, they believe. The essential task of Christianity today is to offer a way to heal the dualism between science and religion, soul and cosmos, psyche and spirit, justice making and celebrating, theology and mysticism, God and us.

Fox notes that creation-centered spirituality is the basic heritage of indigenous peoples throughout human history. All expected the divine "to burst out of anyplace at anytime." Every aspect of their life was oriented around a view of the world informed by creation stories. Creation spirituality is the most ancient tradition in the Bible. The prophetic books and wisdom literature reflect a creation cosmology. Jesus knew this tradition well, and creation theology is reflected in his parables. His hearers recognized him as a wisdom teacher who spoke of ultimate reality with an amazing personal authority.

Ethical values emerge from creation spirituality, a shared vision of common origins and a common human destiny. Ancient tribes maintained their unity through creation stories. The creation story that is being shaped through scientific consensus the world over now binds humanity into a single unified tribe. Not only does this new creation story ground us in the history of how we arrived here, but also it awakens awe and wonder in our existence. Compassion for all of creation flows from an awareness of our interconnectedness.

A sense of gratitude to the Creator is a powerful motivating force for ecological action. An awareness of the extravagance of nature, of our being blessed beyond belief by the gift of life, encourages creativity, liberation, and generosity.

We Believe in Jesus Christ

The heart of Christian ethics is the bold declaration of Jesus that the whole of the Law and the Prophets is "You shall love the Lord your God with all your heart, and with all your soul, and with all your mind, and with all your strength. . . . You shall love your neighbor as yourself" (Mark 12:30).

The essence of God is love. The incarnation of Jesus is evidence of the universal love of God: "For God so loved the world that he gave his only Son. . . . God did not send the Son into the world to condemn the world, but in order that the world might be saved through him" (John 3:16).

To love as God loves is to love not only

> *The rights of sentient animals to be free of excessive pain and to enjoy a modicum of qualitative life, even if their final fate is the human dinner table; the need for "wilderness" habitats to have a balance of predator and prey, if some animals are not to destroy their own carrying capacity; the need to preserve biotic diversity and prevent rapid extinction of species—all these are values that need to be defended. The ethical basis for each of these various values needs to be clarified in a rich tapestry of rights, values, and duties of humans to the other life forms toward which we must assume the responsibility of guardianship.*
>
> —Rosemary Radford Ruether,
> *Gaia and God*

our neighbors (Matt. 4:3), but also to love the biosphere, since God makes the sun to rise and the rain to fall on the evil and the good alike (Matt. 6:15) and cares for sparrows and lilies. Love of neighbor should surely include the creatures of the world, in recognition of our common origins, our mutual interactions, and our shared destiny on earth. Chief Seattle spoke a profound word that we are just now understanding: "If all the beasts were gone, man would die from a great loneliness of spirit."

Jesus lived close to the earth, child of a rural culture, walking everywhere in intimate relationship with nature. He used earth stories to describe his vision of the reign of God he was inaugurating. He spoke of lilies and sparrows and shepherds and sheep and goats and sowing and reaping and gathering into barns. He was compassion incarnate, speaking fondly of earthly matters and engaging daily in simple acts of helping and healing.

The great naturalist Aldo Leopold taught the simple ethical principle that "a thing is right when it tends to preserve the integrity, stability, and beauty of the biotic community. It is wrong when it tends otherwise."[7] The social conscience Jesus taught must in our time be extended beyond people to the biotic community. Our loyalties, our affections, our convictions must be transformed to encompass the natural systems that make all life possible. In short, Christian love requires that we love and respect the earth.

James Nash has made a most thorough and systematic study of the meaning of Christian love in earth care. We might question even the possibility of love under the "tragic conditions of existence in a predatorial biosphere," Nash writes. We live in a world where "every species feeds on and struggles against other species" and "humans must kill and use other life forms" to meet basic survival needs. Even in the face of the "necessary evil" of biological life on the planet, "humans are called to love what God loves, to value what is valued by the Source of Value."[8]

A shallow sentimentalizing of Christian love is unwise in a world where humans are natural predators, and distressingly successful ones at that. But love demands that at least we seek to be "altruistic predators" who seek to "minimize the ecological harm that we inevitably cause and who consume caringly and frugally to retain and restore the integrity of the ecosphere."[9] We are also required to be "creative predators," since "humans alone have evolved peculiar rational, moral, and therefore, creative capacities that enable us alone to serve as responsible representatives of God's interest and values." We are given the charge to protect the biosphere from undue harm, and we were gifted with the intellectual and moral capacity to accept the charge.

It requires a transformed way of thinking to expand the teachings of the Bible on Christian love from interpersonal to ecological spheres. Nash leads us to reflect on the larger meanings of several aspects of Christian love:

◆ Christian love is beneficence, looking not only to one's own interests, but also to the interests of others (Phil. 2:4). It is being "servants to one another" (Gal. 5:13) by seeking "to do good to one another and to all" (1 Thess. 5:15). It is serving Christ by ministering to the hungry, the naked, the lonely, and the prisoners (Matt 25:31-46).

◆ Christian love is other-esteem, valuing, honoring and respecting the integrity of species and the biological systems that sustain them.

◆ Christian love is receptivity. It is "not envious or boastful or arrogant or rude" (1 Cor. 13:45), desiring and receiving the gifts of creation in gratitude. An awe-filled appreciation of the earthy is a powerful force for sustaining the environmental movement.

◆ Christian love is humility, not thinking of ourselves more highly than we ought to think (Rom. 12:3). Love chooses restrained and care-filled ways to minimize risk to the biosphere, recognizing, as Aldo Leopold said, that we are not lords of the universe, but "common citizens with all other creatures."

◆ Christian love is understanding, since we are required to love God with our whole mind (Luke 10:27), hence to love the entire creation, which comes into existence through the love and passion of the Creator. The early debates over the validity of the charge that CFCs and other chemicals harm the ozone layer and that greenhouse gases are causing dangerous global warming illustrate the need for solid research. Without knowledge, the emerging capacity of the human family to do unintentional harm grows.

◆ Christian love is communion, which "binds everything together in perfect harmony (Col. 3:14). It seeks the "unity of the Spirit in the bond of peace" (Eph. 4:3). It is the pursuit of "what makes for peace and for mutual upbuilding" in community (Rom. 14:19).[10]

Looking, then, at the rich fabric of Christian love, we can see how important it is that we retrain our minds to see the neighbor whom we love as the entire biosphere. That includes all of the creatures given by a gracious God for our enjoyment and sustenance. To love God with heart, soul, mind, and strength is to love all that God loves, all that God declared "very good."

It is vital that we see Christian love and justice as organically bound together. In the Hebrew Scriptures, God is seen as the "lover of justice" (Ps. 99:4; Isa. 30:18; 61:8; Jer. 9:24). God exercises justice for the oppressed (Ps. 146:7) and liberates the slaves (Exod. 2:23-24). The covenant with Noah, cherished by Jews and Christians alike, assures the believer that the steadfast love of God extends to all creatures of the earth. Natural forces are dependable and predictable because God's love is steadfast. Does this not mean, then, that the creatures of the earth, being loved of God, have a just claim on human beings to protect them and their habitats?

The New Testament writers assume and expand on the intimate relationship between love and justice, seen clearly in the Hebrew Scriptures. They saw Jesus standing in the prophetic tradition of Isaiah, Amos, and Hosea when he denounced those who "tithe mint, dill, and cummin, and have neglected the weightier matters of the law: justice and mercy and faith. It was these you ought to have practiced without neglecting the others" (Matt. 23:23; Luke 11:42). The reign of God, the core of Jesus' teachings, is the fulfillment of the prophetic vision of justice, tempered with mercy and empowered by compassion in the ministry of our Lord. The reign of God envisions harmony among all the creatures of the earth and the redemption of the entire world.

At the insistence of the developing nations, the UN Earth Summit in Brazil became UNCED, the UN Conference on the Environment and *Development*. On behalf of the poor of the world, leaders of developing nations demanded recognition that global poverty and environmental degradation feed on each other. The joint statement, which we issued from the United Methodist and Brazilian Methodist delegations, focused on this recognition. Lifting up issues the delegates from the United States were trying to block, we condemned the huge arms burden the human family carries—the inequitable distribution of the world's resources and the failure of nations to empower women, who are major food producers in many poor countries. We called for eco-justice for indigenous and ethnic peoples around the world. We challenged lifestyles of conspicuous consumption, which waste the earth's precious resources. We called for the transformation of the global economy.

We spoke from the tradition of Christian love, shaped by the demands of justice for all. We spoke from the awareness that we will have no peace on the earth until we have peace with the earth. We will have no peace with the earth until the human family learns to live together in justice and harmony with creation. I learned recently that the symbol for "peace" in Chinese is a combination of *ho*, "grain," and *ping*, "equitable distribution." Together they spell *hoping* in English. The hope for peace is justice, not alone among members of the human family, but biotic justice as well.

Jonathan Schell wrote in relation to the nuclear crisis: "We will not be saved by our fear. We will be saved by the power of an uncommon love." In the Bronx Zoo, one comes upon a plaque that reads: "In the end, we will preserve only what we love. We will love only what we understand. We will understand only what we are taught." The sacred responsibility of Christians is to teach that special knowledge that the earth belongs to a loving God and to embody that uncommon love, which will save us all.

We Believe in the Holy Spirit

In tribal societies from the dawn of human community, the divine is experienced as a pervasive, diffuse spirit presence throughout the earth and all natural events. The world of the mysterious is intimately involved in human experience. The divine presence may be suddenly revealed in every tree, rock, stream, or mountain. The propitiation of resident spirits through appropriate rituals is considered essential for survival and well-being.

Hebrew spirituality introduced an alternative consciousness, which is expanding yet today wherever animistic faiths meet ethical monotheism. In villages in sub-Saharan Africa the struggle continues. With the coming of Christianity, the psychic and spiritual universe is cleansed of local spirits and demons whose capricious and potentially dangerous presence must be tamed through ritual. In their place emerges an awareness of one unifying, liberating, guiding, and nourishing Spirit. For the Jews, this is *nephesh*, "the breath of life." For Christians, it is the Holy Spirit.

Christians experience the mystery and majesty of the one true God pervading all reality. "The world is filled with the glory of God!" the psalmists sang over and over again. The intimate presence of the Spirit of God is revealed not only through signs in nature, but also in the flow of human history. A powerful spiritual force liberated the Israelites from slavery in Egypt (Exodus 3), molded them into a unified people (Deut. 32:63), and disciplined them when they were unfaithful.

Feminist theologians are helping us to appreciate the Jewish wisdom literature in a new light. Wisdom literature reveals the Spirit of God as a feminine presence in the cosmos. The Holy Spirit is a compassionate, tender, nurturing force. Wisdom, personified and often worshiped as Sophia among Greek-speaking people, was seen as the "mother of all humanity" (Wis. 7:12). She is the source of all creativity, all birthing of creation. She is the spirit that hovers over the waters and brings order into the primordial chaos (Genesis 1).

It was this maternal Spirit that descended upon Jesus at his baptism (Mark 1:10) and anointed him for his ministry of compassionate service and salvation (Luke 4). The forty days and forty nights he spent in the wilderness were a period of discernment, as Jesus waited upon the Spirit to reveal the special nature of his ministry. The infant church was born at Pentecost as this same energizing and empowering Spirit overcame the demoralization of the crucifixion and convinced the disciples that Jesus yet lived as the cosmic Christ. The apostles, nurtured on the Hebrew Scriptures, would have recognized the Spirit as a special visitation of *nephesh*, the powerful breath of God that brought creation to birth.

The Holy Spirit is the source of all attraction in creation, from the subatomic to the cosmic levels, the great unifying force. Modern physicists speak of "enchantment," which draws subatomic particles to each other, shapes the suns and planets out of cosmic dust and holds them in orbit around each other, causes plants to reach for the sun, and lovers of all species to find each other for the creation of new life. The enchantment of the Spirit holds all creation together in "one nurturing, enveloping embrace."

The transcendent God, then, is immanent throughout all creation. We live in a "sacramental universe." We are "priests of a cosmic sacrament," as Eastern Ortho-

> *Do we not already sing our love for and obligation to the land of the free and the home of the brave? Yes, but just what and whom do we love? Certainly not the soil, which we are sending helter-skelter downriver. Certainly not the waters, which we assume have no function except to turn our turbines, float barges, and carry off sewage. Certainly not the plants, of which we exterminate whole communities without batting an eye. Certainly not the animals, of which we have already extirpated many of the largest and most beautiful species.*
>
> —Aldo Leopold,
> *A Sand County Almanac*

dox theologians teach. The earth is holy, the "only biospiritual planet we know." The values and norms that guide us are informed by "a reverence for the material out of which we were born," which nourishes us, delights us, and communicates to us a sense of sacred presence. Ecological ethics emerge from a sense of the mysterious presence of the Holy Spirit in nature. Wonder and awe at the beauty and life-giving properties of nature make us indignant at the exploitation and destruction of the earth's resources and its inhabitants.

Aldo Leopold describes with elegance the sacredness of nature. *The earth is alive,* he insists. Everything in the universe has a phenomenal, or visible, appearance and a noumenal, or spiritual, essence. The earth is an organism that pulsates with life, and "a moral being respects a living thing." The destruction of the "land" or the biosphere is wrong in the same sense that the destruction of another human being is wrong. We sense that Aldo Leopold was in touch with the Holy Spirit in creation as he wrote:

The song of a river ordinarily means the tune that waters play on rock, root, and rapid.

> *It is inconceivable to me that an ethical relation to land can exist without love, respect, and admiration for the land, and a high regard for its value. By value, I of course mean something far broader than mere economic value; I mean value in the philosophical sense.*
>
> —Aldo Leopold,
> *A Sand County Almanac*

... This song of the waters is audible to every ear, but there is other music in these hills, by no means audible to all. To hear even a few notes of it you must first live here for a long time, and you must know the speech of hills and rivers. Then on a still night, when the campfire is low and the Pleiades have climbed over rimrocks, sit quietly and listen for a wolf to howl, and think hard of everything you have seen and tried to understand. Then you may hear it—a vast pulsing harmony—its score inscribed on a thousand hills, its notes the lives and deaths of plants and animals, its rhythms spanning the seconds and the centuries.[11]

Leopold helps us once more to exclaim with Jacob: "Surely the LORD is in this place—and I did not know it! . . . How awesome is this place! This is none other than the house of God, and this is the gate of heaven" (Gen. 28:16-17).

OUR BIBLICAL MANDATE

The Old Testament

In the beginning when God created the heavens and the earth, the earth was a formless void and darkness covered the face of the deep, while a wind from God swept over the face of the waters. Then God said, "Let there be light"; and there was light. And God saw that the light was good. . . . Then God said, "Let us make humankind in our image, according to our likeness; and let them have dominion over the fish of the sea, and over the birds of the air, and over the cattle, and over all the wild animals of the earth, and over every creeping thing that creeps upon the earth."

So God created humankind in his image,
in the image of God he created them;
male and female he created them.

God blessed them, and God said to them, "Be fruitful and multiply, and fill the earth and subdue it; and have dominion over the fish of the sea and over the birds of the air and over every living thing that moves upon the earth." . . . The LORD God took the man and put him in the garden of Eden to till it and keep it. (Gen. 1:1-4, 26-28; 2:15)

Then God said to Noah and to his sons with him, "As for me, I am establishing my covenant with you and your descendants after you, and with every living creature that is with you, the birds, the domestic animals, and every animal of the earth with you. . . . God said, "This is the sign of the covenant that I make between me and you and every living creature that is with you, for all future generations: I have set my bow in the clouds, and it shall be a sign of the covenant between me and the earth. (Gen. 9:8-10, 12)

Then the LORD answered Job out of the whirlwind:

.   .   .   .

"Where were you when I laid the foundation of the earth?
Tell me, if you have understanding.
Who determined its measurements—surely you know!

.   .   .   .

"Have you entered into the springs of the sea,
or walked in the recesses of the deep?
Have the gates of death been revealed to you,

or have you seen the gates of deep darkness?
Have you comprehended the expanse of the earth?
    Declare, if you know all this."
(Job 38:1, 4-5, 16-18)

You visit the earth and water it,
    you greatly enrich it;
the river of God is full of water;
    you provide the people with grain,
    for so you have prepared it.
You water its furrows abundantly,
    settling its ridges,
softening it with showers,
    and blessing its growth.
You crown the year with your bounty;
    your wagon tracks overflow with richness.
The pastures of the wilderness overflow,
    the hills gird themselves with joy,
the meadows clothe themselves with flocks,
    the valleys deck themselves with grain,
    they shout and sing together for joy.
(Ps. 65:9-13)

Bless the LORD, O my soul.
    O LORD my God, you are very great.
You are clothed with honor and majesty,
    wrapped in light as with a garment.
You stretch out the heavens like a tent,
    you set the beams of your chambers on the waters,
you make the clouds your chariot,
    you ride on the wings of the wind,
you make the winds your messengers,
    fire and flame your ministers.

.   .   .   .

O LORD, how manifold are your works!
    In wisdom you have made them all.
(Ps. 104:1-4, 24)

Woe to him who builds his house by unrighteousness,
    and his upper rooms by injustice;
who makes his neighbors work for nothing,
    and does not give them their wages;

.   .   .   .

Did not your father eat and drink

and do justice and righteousness?
Then it was well with him.
He judged the cause of the poor and needy;
then it was well.
Is not this to know me?
says the LORD.
(Jer. 22:13, 15-16)

The New Testament

" 'You shall love the Lord your God with all your heart, and with all your soul, and with all your mind, and with all your strength.' The second is this, 'You shall love your neighbor as yourself.' There is no other commandment greater than these." (Mark 12:30-31)

"Therefore I tell you, do not worry about your life, what you will eat or what you will drink, or about your body, what you will wear. Is not life more than food, and the body more than clothing? Look at the birds of the air; they neither sow nor reap nor gather into barns, and yet your heavenly Father feeds them. . . . And why do your worry about clothing? Consider the lilies of the field, how they grow; they neither toil nor spin, yet I tell you, even Solomon in all his glory was not clothed like one of these." (Matt. 6:25-26, 28-29)

He is the image of the invisible God, the firstborn of all creation; for in him all things in heaven and on earth were created, things visible and invisible, whether thrones or dominions or rulers or powers—all things have been created through him and for him. . . . For in him all the fullness of God was pleased to dwell, and through him God was pleased to reconcile to himself all things, whether on earth or in heaven, by making peace through the blood of his cross. (Col. 1:15-16, 19-20)

NOTES

1. Wesley Granberg-Michaelson, in an article in *Sojourners* (February/March 1990).
2. John McPhee, *The Control of Nature* (New York: Farrar, Straus Giroux, 1989), front flyleaf.
3. Ibid., p. 7.
4. Marc Reisner, *Cadillac Desert*, rev. ed. (New York: Penquin Books, 1993), p. 485.
5. Ibid., p. 486.
6. *The Book of Resolutions of The United Methodist Church* (Nashville: The United Methodist Publishing House, 1996).
7. Aldo Leopold, *A Sand County Almanac* (New York: Ballantine Books, 1970), p. 262.
8. James Nash, *Loving Nature* (Nashville: Abingdon Press, 1991), pp. 139, 141.
9. Ibid., p. 147.
10. See ibid., p. 152.
11. Aldo Leopold, quoted in *Companion to A Sand County Almanac*, by J. Baird Callicott, ed. (Madison: University of Wisconsin Press, 1987), p. 166.

Study Guide

Questions for Reflection

How do the forces that are degrading the environment threaten human rights?

Can you describe the interlocking relationships between global poverty and environmental damage?

Do you agree with the Worldwatch Institute charge that the military is the single largest threat to the environment?

In what ways do Christian theology and practice encourage ecological abuse?

What are some limitations to the Christian doctrine of stewardship of the earth?

Do you agree that we can defend environmental action in traditional Christian terms?

How does the teaching of Jesus that love of God and neighbor is the central commandment guide us in environmental action?

Suggestions for Local Church Study/Action

◆ Organize study groups for youth and adults, using some of the excellent resources now available. (See the "Selected Resources" section.) Place copies of study materials in the church library for others to check out.

◆ Encourage the pastor to use liturgical materials and prayers offered in the "Selected Resources" section.

◆ Urge the congregation to arrange for a total church audit. Adopt such earth-friendly actions as recycling all materials from worship, office, classrooms, and kitchen; eliminate the use of polystyrene and aerosols; install low-flow aerator faucets and water-saving commodes; do an energy audit with the local power company and renovate the church building as recommended; remembering the emerging research linking dioxin to breast cancer, use only dioxin-free paper goods, including unbleached coffee filters. (See the "Selected Resources" section at the end of chapter 5.).

◆ Encourage parishioners to join environmental groups such as the Audubon Society and the Sierra Club. Purchase subscriptions to their publications for the church library. Join them in recommended legislative action.

◆ Take field trips to discover environmental hazards in the community, with special attention to their impact on low-income and racial/ethnic groups. Create or join neighborhood coalitions to demand remedial actions. Order the *Environmental Racism Information* packet from the General Board of Church and Society of The United Methodist Church, 100 Maryland Ave. N.E., Washington, D.C. 20002 (202-488-5600).

◆ Encourage parishioners to join in community gardening, on church grounds if possible. Share surplus produce with needy people in the church or the community. Consider leading the congregation into contracting with a local farmer to grow produce in a consumer-grower cooperative.

Selected Resources

Video
Love the Earth and Be Healed—a series of six half-hour videotapes, with leader guides, on various facets of the environmental crisis. Noted ecologists, theologians, and community activists discuss their involvement and the values that motivate them.

Titles are *Facing Our Dilemmas*; *In This Web Together*; *How Much Is Enough?*; *Loving Nature: Not in Anybody's Backyard!*; and *Celebrating the Earth*. Tape #5 is especially relevant to environmental racism and human rights. Order from EcuFilm, 810 Twelfth Ave. S., Nashville, TN 37203 (800-251-4091 or 615-242-6277). Check to see if your United Methodist Annual Conference film library has copies; if not, encourage a purchase.

Study/Action Resources
From the National Council of the Churches of Christ in the USA

God's Earth Our Home—a packet of materials for congregational study and action on environmental and economic justice. It has been distributed to thousands of congregations.

It's God's World: Christians, the Environment, and Climate Change—written by Vera K. White, this is a helpful guide to a five-session study on global warming

Order these resources from Environmental Justice Resources, National Council of the Churches of Christ in the USA, P.O Box 968, Elkhart, IN 46515 (800-762-0965 or 219-264-3102).

From the General Board of Church and Society of The United Methodist Church

Hope for the Earth, Sharon Delgado—this handbook for Christian environmental groups, was first published by the California-Nevada Conference. It is a study in ten sessions, based on the Wesleyan tradition. The foundation of the study is the Word of God as "revealed in Scripture, illumined by tradition, vivified in personal experience, confirmed by reason"—the Wesleyan quadrilateral. Order from Service Department, General Board of Church and Society, The United Methodist Church, 100 Maryland Ave. NE, Washington, D.C. 20002 (800-967-0880).

101 Ways to Save the Earth—it will be impossible to say that there is nothing you can do after reading this classic checklist of possibilities for environmental action. Order from Service Department, General Board of Church and Society, The United Methodist Church, 100 Maryland Ave. NE, Washington, D.C. 20002 (800-967-0880).

Other Sources
Earth Covenant Church—edited by Susan Gray, dedicated environmentalist who was present with us at the UNCED "Earth Summit" in Brazil, this study was published by the West Michigan Conference. It is an excellent guidebook for congregational worship, study, and action. In addition to liturgical and prayer resources and tips on how to organize the congregation, it includes an "Environmental Theology Curriculum" in four sessions. Order from Susan Gray, Learning Resource Center, Michigan Area, United Methodist Church, P.O Box 6247, Grand Rapids, MI 49506 (616-459-4503).

126

Let the Earth be Glad—probably the most extensive packet of resources available to help congregations to care for the earth. Prepared for those who identify themselves as evangelicals, it should appeal to Christians from a broad range of theological persuasions. Materials for worship, sermon preparation, study groups, and retreats, along with a stewardship audit for church buildings, are organized into four attractive booklets. Order from Evangelical Environmental Network, 10 East Lancaster Avenue, Wynnewood, PA 19096-3495 (610-645-9392).

Books

Loving Nature, James A. Nash (Nashville: Abingdon Press, 1991)—Nash is the Executive Director of the Churches' Center for Theology and Public Policy in Washington, D.C. He has written an excellent study of Christian ecological ethics. He shows how Christian theology offers a strong foundation for environmental action. This is the most thorough discussion I know of on the meaning of Christian love for guiding earth care. It is excellent for extended congregational study.

The End of Nature, Bill McKibben (New York: Anchor Doubleday, 1990)—this book is "a kind of song for the wild, a lament for its loss, and a plea for its restoration." The author contends that our traditional image of pristine nature untouched by human hands is lost forever. The air we breathe, the water we drink, the forests we enjoy, the entire biosphere is altered by the human presence: "We have built a greenhouse, a human creation, where once there bloomed a sweet and lovely garden."

A Sand County Almanac, Aldo Leopold (New York: Ballantine Books, 1970)—first published in 1949, this is one of the most beautiful hymns of praise to nature, a classic ranking with the writings of Henry David Thoreau and John Muir. For a long time out of print, it came to my attention through Judy Lyons of Madison, Wisconsin, who found a worn copy in a used-book store. Now it is readily available in most bookstores. Read it for daily devotions, along with your favorite psalms.

Cadillac Desert, rev. ed., Marc Reisner (New York: Penquin Books, 1993)—the story of the struggle for water in the American West—of rivers diverted and damned, of political corruption, of ecological and economic disaster. It is a stern warning that the dramatic economic growth of the 100 years in the West is not sustainable. It rests uneasily on a foundation of arrogant disregard for the forces of nature.

Gaia and God, Rosemary Radford Ruether (San Francisco: HarperSanFrancisco, 1992)—examining Western patriarchal tradition from an ecofeminist perspective, Ruether, of Garrett-Evangelical Seminary, sees the work of eco-justice and the work of spirituality as interrelated. This is a marvelously stimulating development of a theology of earth care from the feminist perspective, worthy of an extended, all-church study.

Chapter 5

Confronting Domination Systems: Patriarchy

Everyone is entitled to all the rights and freedoms set forth in this Declaration, without distinction of any kind, such as race, color, sex, language, religion, political or other opinion, national or social origin, property, birth or other status.

—Universal Declaration of Human Rights

The churches' own implication in militarism, racism, sexism, and materialism requires a deeply penitent approach to peacemaking.

—In Defense of Creation

It was Christmas 1979. Our clergy delegation was on its way to Ghom in Iran to bring Christmas prayers for peace to the Ayatollah Khomeini. The whole world was watching with tense fascination as a handful of militant students held the U.S. Embassy in Teheran hostage. A nation was collapsing. Fifty thousand graves in the Beheshti Zahra cemetery in south Teheran bore testimony to the scope of the agony. Two colossal superpowers armed with a million Hiroshimas stood glaring at each other across the Iranian frontier.[1]

During the months of the hostage crisis, we observed the growing rage of a frustrated helpless giant, the most powerful nation on earth. The polls showed an escalating public will to rearm the United States. A president with a pre-nuclear age mentality was elected on a promise to show the world we could not be pushed around. The United States set out on the greatest peacetime arms build-up in history, at a cost that threatened to bankrupt the nation.

Who were the men in charge of our foreign policy? During our involvement in the Iranian crisis, we observed the most blatantly arrogant behavior on the part of senior government officials. At a sensitive time, when careful diplomacy could have eased dangerous tensions, we saw only a bellicose, ignorant contempt for the Iranian people and their culture. Language and actions designed to humiliate them only provoked further alienation, fear, and hostility.

I said to Iranian scholar Dr. Thomas Ricks, our interpreter on two trips to troubled Iran, "Tom, doesn't our State Department have access to Iranian specialists to advise them on ways to negotiate with these people?" Tom replied, "Yes, but senior people don't listen to them. The people who rise to the top of our foreign policy establishment must prove their macho toughness. They have to show that they are ruthless enough even to push the nuclear button if necessary." Clearly these are *unbalanced people*. Where do they come from? How did they rise to take charge of a great nation in a time of crisis?

The United States is a violent nation today. Domestic violence grows. Vicarious satisfaction of hostile impulses creates a vast market for TV violence. A superheated competitive economic system builds on a philosophy of social Darwinism. It bleeds the poor and the weak and frustrates the dreams of millions of young people. Even the most reasonable public figures, fearing the "wimp factor" must prove their toughness in political campaign rhetoric. Our answer to the tragedy of drug abuse and urban violence is to build more prisons. A promise to "get tough on crime" garners votes in national campaigns.

Our foreign policy floats on a boiling cauldron of free-floating aggression and homicidal impulse overlaid with a veneer of civilized gentility. Anger triggered in a time of international crisis, reinforced by demagogic leaders and sensationalist television programs, can make us a menace to ourselves and to the rest of the world. Our staunchest allies often fear our instability and unpredictability in times of crisis.

It was in such an atmosphere that the Council of Bishops of The United Methodist Church believed it imperative to ask the United Methodist people to reflect again upon the world we are creating. The Council was sobered by scientific discussions that led to the possibility of nuclear winter. Suddenly it was clear that cults of toughness nurtured by primitive survival fears and inflamed by national chauvinism could threaten the future not only of the human family, but of the biosphere as well. The Worldwatch Institute solemnly warned us that ecological degradation worsened by the runaway arms race and thoughtless industrial development could become the equivalent of a "nuclear winter in slow motion."

In the study *In Defense of Creation*, the Council highlighted some of the forces that fed the flames of violence. An intemperate chauvinistic rhetoric both accompanied and perpetuated cold war animosities and rivalries. The growing influence of the military-industrial-political-scientific-educational-recreational-media-religious complex had taken on a demonic life of its own. In the fashion of domination systems, it drew the energies of otherwise decent people into its vast maw. Greed, lust for power, and the values of military bureaucracies worked together to frighten the American people into supporting aggressive foreign policies and extravagant military spending.

The members of the Council of Bishops prayed that the Methodist people might become evangelists of *shalom*. We urged the people to join together in a new covenant of peacemaking, "embracing all neighbors near and far, all friends and enemies, and becoming defenders of God's good creation, and to pray without ceasing for peace in our time."

In preceding chapters, we have seen the devastating impact on human rights inflicted by domination systems. The global economy is organized to deny basic survival rights to millions of the marginalized. War and preparations for war drive tens of millions into refugee camps. War kills the innocent through starvation and disease as surely as through land mines and missiles. Military systems keep in power oppressive and exploitative governments. Environmental degradation, spread by poverty and war, drives millions to the brink of starvation and deprives future generations of the right to life.

It is no accident that women and children are the primary victims of domination systems. Male power elites, trained in the attitudes and practices of patriarchal domination, do not hesitate to deprive the weakest among us of every social and political right.

The causes of cultural violence are many and complex. No miracle drug is available to assure instant relief. The pyramid of violence corrupts the very bone and sinew of every society. No society is wholly immune. Violence is an ancient curse upon humanity. At the top of the pyramid of violence are weapons of mass destruction—nuclear, chemical, and biological. At the center of the pyramid, the arms race in conventional weaponry grows in magnitude and lethal impact. At the base of the pyramid, the pathological fascination with handguns in the United States puts deadly force into the hands of millions of citizens. Household weapons proliferate, wounding and killing curious children and family members mistaken for intruders. Even our schools become armed camps.

Meanwhile, the mass media glorify violence, feeding and magnifying the readiness to see brute force as the answer to all grievances. The psychological seeds of violence are sown in families for whom abusive behavior is the accepted way of life. Violence must be challenged at every level—families, schools, communities, and governments.

Often overlooked in this scenario is the impact of patriarchal systems. *Domination systems of all sorts root in patriarchy.*

SEXISM AND MILITARISM

One of the more persuasive critiques of the Council of Bishops' nuclear study *In Defense of Creation* came from Dr. Janice Love, Professor of Political Science at the University of South Carolina and a member of the Central Committee of the World Council of Churches. She was quoted in the church press as saying it was a sexist document, which she promptly denied. In fact, she expressed deep appreciation for the courage and wisdom shown by the Council of Bishops as they confronted war-making systems.

Love contended that the Council overlooked one of the most pervasive social forces feeding violence and militarism in Western cultures: "the fundamental symbiosis between sexism and the war system." Patriarchy is the sociosexual foundation of war-making systems, not only in the United States, but also in all of the militarized nation-states. The great power struggle, the "two scorpions in a bottle" syndrome, which caused such massive suffering around the globe and threatened the future of the biosphere, was conflict among male power elites. They fed each other's paranoia and threatened catastrophic destruction if their patriarchal privileges were challenged. Where do these men come from?

Violence-prone men are nurtured in patriarchal institutions that systematically train young people in sharply defined roles. Certain functions are seen as men's work and others as women's work. More value, greater meaning, and richer compensation are given to the work of men. Women are taught to define their individual lives in relationship to a dominant male. They owe him emotional support and loyalty. From him they expect protection and support. In his reflected light, they trace the shape of their own identity.

The heart of Love's analysis is that both positive (authentic) and negative (distorted) masculine and feminine values are available to all human beings. What are those values?

> Positive feminine values are interpersonal, humane, and relationship-oriented traits such as cooperation, caring, equality, fairness, love and affirmation of diversity. Positive masculine values are often more abstract and institutional and have to do with reason, autonomy, assertiveness, and worldly competence. Negative feminine values accentuate dependence, submission, accommodation, and wiles. Negative masculine values emphasize domination, aggression, competitiveness and hierarchy.[2]

Patriarchal cultures are designed to reinforce, to teach, and even to enforce negative feminine values in women and negative masculine values in men. Both men and women are thus prevented from growing into their full potential as whole human beings in creative and productive relation to one another. What is the relationship between this pervasive sex-role socialization and war-making systems?

> Militarism, war, and the war system depend on the accentuation of negative masculine values and the suppression of positive feminine values, just like patriarchy does. Therefore, patriarchy may well be a fundamental cause of this social violence, the root of both sexism and war. Allowing our psyches, culture, and societal institutions to suppress, and, for some, to destroy positive feminine values of cooperation, caring and affirmation of diversity, while glorifying negative masculine values of aggression, competitiveness, and domination, we nurture and perpetuate violent systems and behavior that reaps widespread destruction and may ultimately end life as we know it on this planet.[3]

While nuclear war could be the final insane outcome of patriarchy, "the structural violence of poverty, racial oppression, unemployment, environmental degradation, and sexual abuse claims its casualties every day."

Janice Love's analysis parallels the penetrating work of Betty Reardon in her insightful volume *Sexism and the War System*. Reardon explores the relationship between women's issues and peace and justice. She has been engaged for a number of years in reflection upon the roles of women in the structural transformation required for the dream of a just peace to thrive. The special insights and gifts women could bring to peacemaking are blocked precisely because women's oppression and society's militarization are organically interrelated. Sexism is a major contributor to the world survival crisis in its essential elements—war, poverty, and ecological degradation.

The root causes of war emerge from the human psyche. The major transformational task is to explore and to change the systems that shape the psyche, which socialize men to be warriors and women to be victims or surrogate enemies. Neither sexism nor the war system is instinctual or innate; we are trained to our roles. Both sexism and socially sanctioned violence are learned behaviors and, therefore, subject to intentional change.

Sociological studies point to several key elements in the relationship between sexism and violence in patriarchal cultures:

1. *Rigid sex-role socialization increases aggression among males.* What is the impact of the personality distortions imposed by child-care systems that differentiate sharply between masculine and feminine roles and identities? They increase male frustration, social distancing, alienation, and hence aggression. The socialization of boys leads to more emotional deprivation, more pressure to reject the gentler attributes allowed to women, more performance demands. It is not surprising that the resulting frustration leads to aggression. Moreover, men are permitted to act out anger, while women are required to suppress it. Men are encouraged to be more competitive, even to the point of exploiting others or attacking them to achieve success.

2. *The oppression of women is the first and most extensive form of structural oppression.* For both boys and girls, "the first socially encountered other, a person they perceive as being different from themselves is usually of the other sex."[4] In patriarchal cultures, an element of threat and fear often becomes identified with the perception of

> *The Aztecs sacrificed the flower of their civilization's youth to appease their gods and keep the national order in place. For centuries, we have sacrificed ours to the gods of war. Now a scientific and military priesthood seeks to deter the change in the "natural order" that promises to transcend the social difference between men and women.*
>
> —Betty Reardon

"otherness." It is this fear of diversity that finally gives rise to the notion of the "enemy," upon whom we project the negative attributes we deny in ourselves.

Sexist alienation of male from female results from the rejection—even to the point of despisement to assure the rejection of "feminine" characteristics in boys and men and "masculine" characteristics in women. Sexist alienation is, I believe, a fundamental basis for alienation in general and negative otherness perceptions in particular. The development of enemy images, indeed, might not be possible were not all human beings socialized into negative otherness from birth.[5]

Violence against gay men and lesbians no doubt finds its psychological roots in this early childhood nurture. People of a homosexual orientation are "different," hence dangerous. They may come to be seen as an "enemy," to be oppressed, harassed, and attacked.

3. *The shaping of the masculine mind to be precise, technical, and logical leads to the "masculinization of technology" and the implements of war.* For several decades, more than 40 percent of the scientists and engineers in the United States have been at work on the creation of destructive weapons and their supporting technical systems. This is predominantly men's work, since men are trained selectively to think in pragmatic, straight-line logical and instrumental patterns.

Helen Caldicott relates an interview with Joe Weitzenbaum, professor of computer science at MIT. Asked why so many scientists and engineers work willingly on systems of possible genocide, he replied, "Do you know why? It's incredible fun!" The intellectual challenge of solving the technical problems in MIRVing a missile or creating a monstrous new bomb overrides any qualms they may feel about the intended use of such contraptions. No wonder Caldicott says, "We must take the toys away from the boys!"

> *Many men remain intoxicated by violence and potential violence. They watch with fascination the killing power apparent in the speed of military planes—and the slow awesome might of Trident submarines. All their lives they have been seduced by the John Wayne image—the tough, macho hero who shows no emotions while he kills people and who is always right.*
>
> —Helen Caldicott, in Alan Geyer, *The Idea of Disarmament*

THE PLAYING FIELDS OF ETON

It was often said that the playing fields of Eton prepared generations of young British men for their warrior roles in the military control of the colonies. The empire on which the sun never set was created and protected by young men specially trained to their task. They were taken from their homes at an early age, thus assuring emotional deprivation and detachment. This allowed the formalization of relationships into carefully crafted rules and objective tasks. They were nurtured in all-male environments where prestige and acceptance depended on physical prowess on the soccer field, leadership skills in a paramilitary structure, and intellectual excellence in technical fields. It was all designed to support the domination systems of an exploitative, highly militarized colonial power.

What is the modern equivalent of the playing fields of Eton in industrialized cultures? Some find the modern equivalent in video games, elaborate CD-ROM war games, and the cosmic battles of the future portrayed in science fiction films and television programs. These media are preparing the consciousness and motor skills required for the high-tech, push-button warfare upon which modern military systems increasingly depend. A dispassionate, competitive gaming atmosphere is designed to disguise the human suffering and horrible scenes created at a distance by button-pushing warrior heroes.

Pilots in Vietnam reminisced about the sense of unreality they felt as they took off from modern bases, unleashed their fury on distant villages, and returned to their golf games and officers' clubs, their uniforms immaculately pressed. Certainly the Persian Gulf War was "the great Nintendo game in the sky." Much of the industrial world exulted as they watched the display on CNN. They saw "smart bombs" dive into buildings and bunkers, scarcely pausing to think of the grisly scenes of carnage inside. As Iraqi troops and equipment fleeing Kuwait along an exposed highway were systematically destroyed, pilots commented, "It was like a turkey shoot!"

Some argue that war games are but one symptom of a more pervasive problem. Patriarchal societies create generations of men who are prepared to commit mass murder. Certain pre-arranged cultural signals are calculated to trigger their resolve or their rage in a time of international crisis.

THOU SHALT NOT FEEL

Kenneth Druck, in the book *The Secrets Men Keep*, describes the human cost of rigid male sex-role nurturing:

> We block off entire areas of ourselves, and stamp them "Top Secret," and file them away. And we keep their very existence a secret from wives, girlfriends, children, and buddies. We see these parts of who we are as a threat. Perhaps they embarrass us. Or maybe they fail to confirm a particular image we have set out to project for others.[6]

What are the secrets men keep? They hide their deepest fears and insecurities, as well as many of their fondest dreams. Most growing boys learn at an early age to block out an entire range of feelings. Boys are told again and again: "Don't cry!" "Act like a man!" "Don't be a mommy's boy!" Thus they learn that tenderness, emotional sensitivity, dependence, and vulnerability are not acceptable feelings for "real men." They must strive to be tough, super-rational, aggresssive, self-reliant, competitive. Above all else, they must always be in control.

Watergate conspirator G. Gordon Liddy illustrates the relationship between this cauterization of human feelings and violence in the culture. He is reported to have said: "To be strong, a man must be able to stand utterly alone, able to meet and deal with life relying solely upon his own resources. Once I held my hand in the flame of a candle—just to see how tough I was."

Domestic violence, especially child and spouse abuse by violent men, stems in part from the emotional damage of rigid sex-role socialization. Men who batter fear intimacy with women and tenderness in themselves. Their repressed dependency needs break out in rage. One observer described battering as a substitute for human tears. Having been taught not to cry and that when threatened or hurt they should "fight like a man," they victimize women as a means of exorcising their own forbidden "feminine" feelings.

> *Thou shall not cry.*
> *Thou shall not display weakness.*
> *Thou shall not need affection, gentleness or warmth.*
> *Thou shall comfort but not desire comforting.*
> *Thou shall be needed but not need.*
> *Thou shall touch but not be touched.*
> *Thou shall be inviolate in your manhood.*
> *Thou shall stand alone.*
>
> —"Commandments for Men," in Marc Feigen Fasteau, *The Male Machine*

CULTS OF TOUGHNESS

Marc Feigen Fasteau, in *The Male Machine*, reveals the dangerous consequences when powerful leaders allow their personal need to appear tough to shape foreign policy. The United States blundered into ever-deepening involvement in Vietnam in part because presidents Kennedy, Johnson, and Nixon and their advisers subscribed to the first principles of masculine posturing: Never back away once a line is drawn in the sand. Every battle must be won. Never admit error or defeat. Protect honor at all cost. Never give the appearance of hesitation or weakness. If you do, your opponents will shame you or redouble their efforts to conquer you.

The arms race proceeded far beyond the point of rationality because the ethic of masculinity requires the posturing of toughness, fearlessness, and macho strutting. For decades the drumbeat of bellicose rhetoric among American leaders simply strengthened the supermasculine chest beating among Soviet "Iron-eaters." The result was a dangerous circular syndrome of escalating threats and counterthreats. One fancies that leaders on both sides must have learned their statecraft as little boys playing "King of the hill" or "Cock of the walk" games. Serious negotiations for nuclear arms control were again and again sacrificed to the conspiracies on each side to gain advantage over the other. Solemn treaties to limit the numbers of nuclear weapons were circumvented. The most blatant example was the use of the Salt I Treaty as a ruse to increase the number of warheads on each missile. This cynical ploy resulted in a more dangerous and unstable situation than before. In the words of Marc Fasteau: "Let us begin to talk about what is really going on in the minds of the men who spend our blood and our treasure to save their sacred honor."[7]

ABSTRACT THOUGHT AND THE TECHNO FIX

In a recent forum I attended, a sociologist told us that citizens of the United States are members of a "techno-fix" culture. We believe all human problems have a technological solution. In the early part of this century, for instance, thousands of women were addicted to morphine in a misguided attempt by doctors to treat nervousness and hysteria with chemical means. Heroin was introduced as a supposedly nonaddictive substitute, which led to an new generation of addicts. Modern medicine is so biased toward chemical and mechanical treatment modalities that the preventive strategies of holistic self-care have been seriously neglected. The medical establishment is only now beginning to accept alternative healing methods.

The Strategic Defense Initiative (SDI), aptly dubbed "Star Wars," continues to surface in congressional debates, as though the cold war had never ended. It is an extreme example of trying to solve political and spiritual problems with a techno-fix remedy at a cost of billions of dollars. Carl Sagan testified to the Council of Bishops' Washington, D.C., panel that SDI is "not only a foolish idea; it is a dangerous idea." This speaks to the futile and possibly disastrous destabilizing impact of such a scheme. Some of the motivation behind agitation to resurrect SDI is rather transparent. We can see the obvious commercial interest of arms manufacturers to profit from huge appropriations of public funds, and the hope of some members of Congress to bring the largess into their districts. The deeper motivation is the will to turn from the difficult task of negotiation and reconciliation to the familiar and elusive search for a technological solution.

Betty Reardon describes this problem as the "masculinization of technologies." Men are trained to develop precise, technical, and logical minds. Science and technology are for the most part the province of men, since men are presumed to have the required analytical skills. Further, they are assigned the role of controlling the environment. Women are conditioned to be in touch with the emotions in addition to the rational mind, to sense their environment intuitively, to cultivate relational skills. Shaping masculine perceptions and values into tools for coercion and control has too often guided technological innovation. Its purpose is to enhance the power and prestige of male power elites. The major purpose of military deterrence is to prevent "the liberation of the oppressed, the global achievements of human equality, particularly women's equality."[8]

James Nelson coined the term "abstractionism." It refers to the abstract and hyper-rationalized thought patterns to which men have been nurtured. What he terms "bodily concreteness" is lost as sensitivity to the environment is blunted.

Abstractionism makes possible a distorted, overly simplified, and possibly violent sense of reality. Complex foreign policy issues are forced into a cops-and-robbers, cowboys-and-Indians, ranchers-and-squatters mold. Thousands of people died in Nicaragua because the liberation struggles of a desperately poor and oppressed people were stereotyped as a Communist threat to the Western world. North/South social justice struggles were cast without serious reflection into the category of East/West confrontation. Only military responses were seriously considered.

Abstractionism allows otherwise intelligent men to stand in the ashes of a Vietnamese village and say, "We had to destroy this village in order to save it." Abstractionism allows the stockpiling of a million Hiroshimas and the risking of all higher forms of life on the planet by the ritualistic intoning of the mantra "national security." Abstractionism allows for the degradation of air, earth, and water in the name of prosperity. The "rape of the earth" is a fitting description of the toll in human values and the integrity of the biosphere emerging from a perverted sexuality.

Helen Caldicott describes encounters with senior military officers who spoke with great confidence in the technical language of throw-weights and delivery systems, but who flew into a rage as she described in detail the medical consequences. The massive and horrible injuries to millions of men, women, and children that a nuclear interchange would inflict could appropriately be called "the last great epidemic."

Abstractionism makes possible the degrading of language to distort the ethical significance of preparations for high-tech warfare. Bernard Lown of Harvard, upon receiving the Nobel Peace Prize for the International Physicians for the Prevention of Nuclear War, described it well:

> This [nuclear] build-up is like a cancer, the cells of which multiply because they have been genetically programmed to do no other. Pointing nuclear-tipped missiles at entire nations is an unprecedented act of moral depravity. The horror is obscured by its magnitude, by the sophistication of the means of slaughter, and by the aseptic Orwellian language crafted to describe the attack—"delivery vehicles" provide an "exchange" in which the death of untold millions is called "collateral damage."

Abstractionism makes possible the "vocabulary of dispassionate terror": *overkill, megadeath, tolerable death rate, thermal effects, unacceptable damage, assured destruction capability.* Missiles are called "peacemakers." A submarine that can destroy 190 cities is christened with the name of Christ. Small wonder that Alan Geyer could write: "The nuclear arms race has become this generation's severest test of truth. It is zealously promoted with false words, deceptive jargon, pretentious dogmatics, hateful propaganda, and arbitrary bars on access to the truth."[9] Abstractionism makes it possible for brilliant scientists and engineers, trained in hyper-rational, "masculine" thought patterns to do with great efficiency what should never have been done at all.

WOMEN AND WAR

Since military systems are patriarchal in essence, and since war making is uniquely a male preoccupation, the impact on women and children needs to be carefully studied. We might profit from an examination of women as victims, women as warriors, and women as peacemakers.

Women as Victims

Anyone with a television set carries visual memories of the long lines of refugees fleeing from Rwanda into camps in Zaire (now the Congo). More than a million exhausted, frightened people, most of them women and children, fled their country, trying desperately to survive. We watched them later filling the roads as far as the eye could see, straggling back toward their homeland, weak with fear at what they might find there. In that scene we witnessed the nature of modern warfare. Women and children are overwhelmingly the victims of the folly of men at war.

I have seen the refugees in the camps of Sierra Leone and Zimbabwe and Palestine. Eighty percent of them are women, they say. I remember the children of Mozambique in the camps in Zimbabwe. At the clang of a piece of an iron rail, which served as a bell, they would dash to the feeding stations, tin plates clutched in their little hands. I have seen them with their plates balanced precariously on their heads, rough housing with each other. By some miracle they spilled not a grain of precious rice or the dried sardines that made up their one meal a day. I remember them going to school in the shade of a tree. They expected to be there a long time.

I noted in chapter 1 that the just-war ideal of sparing noncombatants in time of war has been flagrantly and deliberately violated throughout this bloody century. Saturation bombing of cities was initiated by the Nazis and quickly copied by the Allies. Who in my generation can forget the horror of London burning or the firebombing of Dresden? Visiting Dresden later, I stood with church leaders of Dresden on a hill overlooking the city. They tearfully described their feelings as they had watched their city burning. As noted earlier, by the time we had dropped the atomic bomb on Hiroshima and Nagasaki, virtually every city in Japan had been destroyed by incendiary bombs, with untold hundreds of thousands of civilian casualties.

In our time we have witnessed mass starvation as a weapon of war. Again and again in North African countries, relief supplies have been deliberately interdicted by warring armies, with women and children the primary victims. On one occasion I went with a small delegation of denominational leaders to El Salvador to protest to President Christiani the withholding of relief supplies. He seemed impressed with our argument that such an act is a gross violation of the Geneva Convention, and promised to discipline his military.

A disturbing image that I will carry with me as long as I live is that of the sniper in Sarajevo being interviewed on television. With a demonic grin, he said, "I especially like to shoot a child in its mother's arms, just to see the look of horror on the mother's face!"

Mass rape as a weapon of war is not new to this century, although it seems to have been systematically employed with a special bestiality in these past decades. During World War II, Jewish, Gypsy, Polish, and Russian women were gang-raped by Nazi soldiers. In revenge, Russian troops raped more than 900,000 women in conquered Berlin. The Japanese army raped the women of Nanking and forced thousands of Korean, Filipino, and Chinese women, interning them in camps to serve as "comfort women."

Once again, this time in Bosnia-Herzegovina, the brutal practice has surfaced. The Women for Women in Bosnia coalition estimates that 50,000 women were ravaged over the months of the war. Their account was recently published in the *Journal of Sacred Feminine Wisdom*, edited by Susan Perz. Zainab Salbi, president of the Bosnian group, explores the meaning of rape as a tool and a weapon of war. She describes it as a "sexual manifestation of aggression," designed to humiliate the men of the enemy camp. It flourishes on the patriarchal notion that a woman is the property of men, to be appropriated or destroyed at will. Salbi writes:

I argue that rape, specifically in wartime, and regardless of the culture of the parties involved, has political, military, and sociological dynamics and implications. Rape in wartime is used to demonstrate the unequal power relations not only between the sexes but also between two opponents. Since a woman is viewed not only as a part of nature, but also as the carrier of her peoples' honor and heritage, the torture inflicted on her through rape is not only meant to rape her body, but also to rape her peoples' identity, heritage, and honor.[10]

Rape is a way not only of demonstrating the soldiers' masculinity, but also of symbolically depriving the defeated soldiers of their machismo. It is often a tool to raise soldiers' morale and assure their bonding. The impregnating of Bosnian Muslim and Catholic women was used to terrorize the population and force them to flee, and thus became a tool of "ethnic cleansing." The especially repugnant practice of impregnating a woman and holding her captive until too late for an abortion was devised to return her to her husband, carrying in her womb a permanent reminder of his humiliation.

Wherever women are victimized by war, it is obvious that innocent children suffer as well. In its publication *State of the World's Children 1992*, UNICEF declared that war on children is "the 20th Century's shame." In the decade of the nineties more than 1.5 million children have been killed in wars, and another 4 million disabled. Many of these children are still being maimed or killed by the millions of land mines scattered across Africa and Asia. Watching television images of crying children separated from their parents in the mass movement of refugees from Rwanda and Burundi reminded us that over 5 million children struggle to survive in refugee camps.

At a lunchtime workshop on Africa at the 1996 General Conference of The United Methodist Church, I heard the delegates from Africa pay heart-felt tribute to the United Methodist Committee on Relief (UMCOR). Their work among the orphans and lost children at the Goma

> *This "war on children" is a 20th century invention. Only 5 percent of the casualties in the First World War were civilians. By the Second World War the proportion had risen to 50 percent. And, as the century ends, the civilian share is normally about 80 percent—most of them women and children. . . . The time has now come for a worldwide public to cry out against this war on children—against those who use the weapons and those who supply them . . . and insist that this appalling stain on the 20th century should not be allowed to seep over into the 21st.*
>
> —*State of the World's Children 1992* (UNICEF)

refugee camp in Zaire (now Congo) saved hundreds of lives. Returning from Goma, Genina Wills, then on the UMCOR staff showed us one of the inexpensive rubber shoes they had purchased for the children. From having walked barefoot over the lava fields of the nearby volcano, the children's feet were bleeding and torn. A German company was able to ship hundreds of thousands of pairs of the shoes to the children of Goma.

Women as Warriors

Women have served in the armed forces of the United States since the Civil War. Usually they have filled positions as nurses, secretaries, cooks, or drivers. Their role as nurses in Korea has been dramatized by the long-running television series "M*A*S*H." During the Persian Gulf War, they were more visible than ever before. Some 20,000 women saw duty there. While largely excluded from combat, they were allowed to launch Patriot missiles, thus participating directly in killing. Today the United States has the largest proportion of women to men in the military of any industrial country.

Women have played significant roles during times of war in all of our conflicts, and especially during the total mobilization of World War II. They have brought food to troops, sewed bandages and hospital sheets, donated blood, and bought War Bonds. During World War II, Rosy the Riveter made possible the massive build-up of armaments, leaving the kitchen to work in the factory. Her picture was on posters all over smalltown America, as a means of encouraging every citizen to "do your part." While women were forced back into the kitchens following the war, it proved impossible to keep them there. The quiet revolution of the two-paycheck marriage was a direct result of wartime mobilization. Some sociologists cite this as the most important cultural transformation in the past fifty years.

Leisa Meyer, Professor of History at the College of William and Mary, who herself trained at the U.S. Air Force Academy, published a recent study: *Creating GI Jane: Sexuality and Power in the Women's Army Corp During World War II*. She believes that serving in the military empowered women to play a key role in the civil rights movements following the war. Struggling against racism and sexism, African American women and men agitated against discrimination in the service. They fought discrimination with letter-writing campaigns, sit-ins, and sit-down strikes. This basic training in methods of social protest eventually enhanced the status of African Americans and all women in the military. Their status within the larger civilian culture was also affected.

The recent reports of rape, sexual assault, and harassment throughout the military have revived a debate over women in the military. Congressman Robert Livingston, who heads the House Appropriations Committee, was quoted in the December 29, 1996, *New York Times* as having said, "The facts indicate that the complete integration of men and women in all aspects of military life has proven to be a disaster." His is a powerful voice, since he heads the congressional committee that oversees military spending.

In the same article, female military officers, along with some male officers and members of Congress, argue that incidents of sexual abuse are a reason to open thousands of combat positions now closed to women. They believe that until women are treated as equals, men will continue to mistreat them. When women are allowed to advance along the three main routes to senior leadership in the military—armor, infantry and field artillery—sexual abuse will stop.

This statement condenses the two main arguments that women should serve in combat positions:

1. *The presence of women will humanize the military.* Betty Friedan insisted that women warriors would be effective in curbing brutality in future wars. After all, women are more sensitive to life. Professor Madeline Morris, in an article in *The Duke Law Journal* in February 1996, went so far as to say that we could reduce military rape rates by integrating women into the military. Their presence would presumably change the norms that make military men so prone to commit rape and other abuses of women.

2. *The inclusion of women in combat roles is an issue of equal opportunity.* In 1981, the National Organization for Women (NOW) filed a legal brief to challenge the all-male military draft registration. Just as women have gained the right to vote, so also they should do compulsory military service, they insisted. It is a civic right and a civic virtue. Women will never be first-class citizens until they have the right to fight. Women suffer long-term psychological and political effects by being excluded from combat. Such exclusion, they say, is an archaic notion. As described in the *New York Times* article, critics responded that this equal-opportunity feminism has been co-opted to validate militarism by perpetuating the "notion that the military is so central to the entire social order that it is only when women gain access to its core that they can hope to fulfill their hopes and aspirations."

I believe that as long as the military functions as the major jobs program in the society, women will have a just claim to full participation. As long as the military is a primary way up and out for young people trapped in poverty, women have a right to equal opportunity within it. As long as the way to promotions into senior ranks is to be "blooded" in combat, women will see exclusion from combat as a glass ceiling blocking their career aspirations.

Feminists can also argue persuasively that modern high-tech warfare has opened up an increasing range of combat positions for which women can qualify. When I was traveling heavily, I grew accustomed to seeing young women pilots guiding huge commercial airliners through the skies. The same young women could have been at the controls of a jet fighter or a military cargo plane. Electronically activated guidance mechanisms do the heavy work. Women are as capable as men in fighting the "Nintendo" type of push-button war we saw in Desert Storm. Our troops killed distant enemies whose agonies they did not have to witness, while themselves standing off far from danger. This is the style of combat for which the Pentagon is preparing for future wars.

We could argue also that modern warfare tends to involve the entire culture. It is difficult to distinguish between women in combat and women on assembly lines creating the weapons or women firing guided missiles at Iraqi targets or women involved in the vast range of behind-the-lines logistical and support functions that most military personnel perform, even at the height of combat. In a permanent warfare culture such as ours has become, all citizens are involved directly or indirectly in war or the preparation for war.

As for the contention that women will transform the culture of the military, I remain skeptical. The same claim was made when women began to be elected to Congress in growing numbers. While a number of women have made outstanding contributions to political life, the promise of an automatic emergence of a "kinder, gentler" political culture has hardly transpired.

My central concern with the integration of women into military culture is this: *Their voices as peacemakers will be muted.* Note that only *after they retired* were the sixty generals and admirals free to declare that nuclear weapons have no strategic military value (see chapter 3). While on active duty, whatever their private thoughts, they were restricted by their military obligations to defend the policies of the moment. Can we expect that women in the military will be any freer to advocate for cutbacks in military expenditures or the phasing out of nuclear weapons?

It is apparent that if women alone must be peacemakers, we will never have peace. Men of goodwill and courage, even within the military, have taken bold steps toward peace at critical moments. Yet women have traditionally played a vital catalytic role in mobilizing others to advocate for an end to war. Their very non-participation in war making has freed them to dream of new futures and to organize to bring them into being. Their experiences as mothers, as reconcilers within the household, and their training in positive feminine values have made them an invaluable asset the culture cannot afford to lose.

Women as Peacemakers

Throughout my ministry the majority of colleagues and friends who have been most effective and faithful in peacemaking have been women. Traveling around the country for years as a general officer of the Church convinced me that it is United Methodist Women who study international affairs in depth and who are the most articulate and committed global citizens.

I participated in interboard schools through the rural Midwestern states during the early 1960s. On a sub-district basis, a team of staff specialists from the several general agencies of the Church would spend several hours in each location. The John Birch Society at the time was poisoning the atmosphere with its paranoid fulminations about the United Nations. UNICEF was portrayed as a Communist front organization. Halloween trick-or-treating for UNICEF was seen as a plot to subvert the children of America. As the representative of our social action agencies, men hostile to our peacemaking activities consistently attacked me. In every place it was the women, many of whom had participated in UN seminars, who came to my rescue. On one occasion, a man stood to attack the UN. His wife pulled on his coattails, saying, "Now, John, you sit down! You don't know a thing in the world about that!"

Serving as a Director of the Women's Division of the General Board of Global Ministries for several years (1984–92) gave me a firsthand understanding of the intensive leadership development programs in which United Methodist Women participate. One of the largest women's organizations in the country, it is the most progressive force among the United Methodist people. Its longstanding commitment to social justice, human rights, racial equality, and peace has earned it the respect of citizens' organizations in many countries. Its schools of missions, national seminars, and quadrennial national assembly have lifted the global horizons and deepened the Christian commitment of hundreds of thousands of women—and not a few men. Women organized for mission have been a powerful force in shaping the policies of the entire denomination. They are influential in defining the priorities of our global and national mission programs.

During a national seminar the theme of militarism was addressed in a seminar. Several hundred women were gathered into table groups. During a period of discussion, each table group reported on the many peacemaking organizations in which the women in that group were active. I came away from that seminar with an overwhelming sense of the power of women to transform society.

> *Arise then, women of this day! Arise, all women who have hearts, whether your baptism be that of water or of tears! Say firmly, "We will not have great questions decided by irrelevant agencies. Our husbands shall not be taken from us to unlearn all that we have been able to teach them of charity, mercy and patience! We women of one country will be too tender of those of another country to allow our sons to be trained to injure theirs. From the bosom of the devastated earth a voice goes up with our own. It says, "Disarm! Disarm!"*
>
> —The original Mother's Day Proclamation 1870

Historical Roots

United Methodist Women stand in a long tradition of women involved in peacemaking. Few remember now that the original Mother's Day Proclamation of 1870 was a ringing call for disarmament.

One of the most accessible recent accounts of women as peacemakers is *Women and War*, by Jeanne Vickers. She writes that the first women's peace societies were established in England in 1820 and in the United States during the 1930s. It was a woman, Bertha von Suttner of Austria, who convinced Alfred Nobel to establish the Nobel Peace Prize. She was the first recipient. Other women who have received this prize include Jane Addams, a U.S. social worker; Emily Greene Balch of Wellesley College in the U.S.; Marie Slodowska Curie, French scientist; Mairesal Corrigan and Betty Williams of Ireland; Alva Myrdal, Swedish economist; Mother Teresa of India; Lady Rama Rao of India; Aung San Suu Kyi, who remains under house arrest in Myanmar (formerly Burma); and Rigoberta Menchu Tum of Guatemala.

Vickers describes an array of women's peace organizations that are active around the world. As early as 1900 an International Peace Bureau was established in Berne, Switzerland, and by 1915 an International Women's Peace Movement was organized. Three women founded the War Resisters League in 1923. In 1932, women collected nine million signatures on a petition sent to the World Disarmament Conference, urging universal disarmament. In 1959, the European Movement of Women Against Nuclear Armament became active in urging a treaty to ban nuclear testing, contributing to the signing of the Partial Test Ban Treaty in 1963.

In recent decades new peace movements have emerged. Among them are Women Strike for Peace, Women's International League for Peace and Freedom, Women for Mutual Security, Churchwomen United, and the Women's World Summit Foundation, to name a representative few. Many other peace organizations have been founded by women in Africa, Asia, the Middle East, Europe, and in Caribbean and Latin American nations.

Some Current Voices

Women's voices and actions have been influential in any number of organizations dedicated to justice, peace, and the integrity of creation. Josephine Pomerance was honored with the creation of an annual award for contributions to disarmament within the UN system. Randall Forsberg led the way in the Nuclear Freeze campaign, and thousands of women made it a global effort. At the Nuclear Non-Proliferation Treaty Renewal Conference at the UN, I met Inga Thorsson, former Swedish Minister of State for Disarmament, who has played a key role in UN disarmament conferences. I have already discussed the amazing career of Helen Caldicott, founder of Physicians for Social Responsibility. Through Choose Peace retreats, I have met a number of women religious of the Roman Catholic Church, usually invisible in the media, but a remarkable force for community renewal in the church.

In preparing *In Defense of Creation*, the Council of Bishops of The United Methodist Church held two days of hearings in Washington, D.C. Some of the most outstanding peacemakers of our time came to testify. In the midst of a superheated, highly militarized industrial society dominated by male power elites, it is important to listen to the voices of women. Let their testimony be a fitting conclusion to this study.

Barbara Green, coordinator of the Public Policy Ministry of the Presbyterian Peacemaking Program, addressed some of the theological issues in the nuclear crisis. She offered four principles for a just peace: (1) a sense of world community reflected in global organizations capable of conflict resolution and capable of coping with global problems; (2) a sense of security based not on military power but on understanding; (3) a sense of dignity and integrity of individuals and a commitment to both social and individual human rights; and (4) social and economic justice and participatory equity in patterns of production and distribution.

Ellen Nissenbaum, Legislative Director of the Center on Budget and Policy Priorities, reminded us that American taxpayers would spend over $275 billion on military programs in 1986. That is more than any year since the end of World War II, including the years of the wars in Korea and Vietnam. It is double the amount spent on military programs just five years earlier. Meant to increase national security, those expenditures contributed to an increasing sense of insecurity among the citizens of the United States. This sharp growth in the military budget drained funds from our economic infrastructure and programs to ensure our collective social well-being. She testified: "This shift in federal spending priorities from domestic programs to military programs is increasing the deficit, hampering our nation's economic productivity, and making it more difficult to solve the persistent problems of long-term and structural unemployment."

Jeanne Vaughn Mattison, Director of the American Committee on East-West Accord, an organization to promote pragmatic business-like relations with the Soviet Union, quoted George Kennan, who said: "There is no issue at stake in our political relations with the Soviet Union, no hope, no fear, nothing to which we aspire, nothing we would like to avoid which could conceivably be worth a nuclear war." Mattison said the quintessential joint venture, the ultimate investment by two great powers is that we not blow each other off the face of the earth. She pointed out that in the very midst of negotiations to limit nuclear weapons, the numbers the military deployed tripled. Only fresh thinking will enable us to get control of the situation. Mattison called it break-set: "It means discarding stale and ineffective approaches and exploring new solutions without preconception—what is called break-set; breaking the mold, thinking anew, fresh. Break-set is exactly what happened when Nixon went to China, when Sadat set foot on Israeli soil, when Apollo and Soyuz rendezvoused in space—and what must happen with the nuclear arms race." Mattison described her involvement in private exploratory break-set conversations with leading Soviet scientists, nuclear arms control specialists, and political leaders, including Gromyko.

Randall Forsberg was the founder and Executive Director of the Institute for Defense and Disarmament Studies and the creative mind behind the Nuclear Freeze campaign. She expressed her conviction that the world will see no solution to the nuclear arms race until the nations begin to "dismantle the entire war system, making cuts in nuclear weapons parallel with constraints and reduction in conventional forces." A narrow focus on curtailing nuclear arms production has failed because it overlooks the most powerful motivation for continuing to produce them—the prevention of conventional wars of the destructive scope of World War I and World War II." She insisted, "Even the strategic intercontinental nuclear forces which we hear much more about are oriented more to deterring conventional war by threatening escalation to nuclear war than to deterring an out-of-the-blue nuclear attack on the cities." In order to reduce the risk of nuclear war, peace advocates must "focus on what must be done to get rid of the conventional war system." This requires narrowing the definition of a just war to one with only one purpose: to defend against a "clear case of externally mounted aggression by another nation." This requires an end to interventionist policies, the closing of foreign military bases, and negotiated reductions of both nuclear and conventional forces to a minimum deterrence level.

Betty Bumpers, founder and president of Peace Links, used her influence as the spouse of a United States Senator to organize thousands of women into a powerful citizens' movement for peace. She said that legislative and administrative policies would change only if enough people organize to demand change: "During the history of the United States we as a people have made fundamental policy changes that have been reversed. The movement for American independence was a gradual movement, as well as abolition of slavery, women's suffrage, the child labor laws, and I can give you many other examples. But once the policies were established there was no turning back. So it must be with nuclear weapons. The recognition that nuclear weapons will ensure our own destruction must lead us to call for a policy change so great that we will never again consider their use, nor create more, nor stockpile those we have." Bumpers urged the churches to be a vital part of a citizens' movement to affect change. We can counter the myth that peacemakers are weakening our country: "The churches have a responsibility to define strength in terms other than nuclear weapons. Our country cannot be strong unless its citizens are well educated and healthy. Our country cannot provide leadership to the world unless we have moral strength, unless we work for justice—unless our economy is strong, not plagued by $200 billion deficits and huge trade imbalances."

Bumpers said that as she speaks to women's groups all over the country, she finds that the technical knowledge men possess often intimidates women. They do not trust their intuitive awareness that the arms race spells disaster. The churches should encourage every citizen to speak out boldly: "As citizens, we must maintain the delicate balance between 'we the people' and our elected leadership guiding this country. You can give peace work credibility and responsibility. There are two important perceptions about people in the peace movement that the church can help to establish. The first is that peace work is patriotic and just, and is work that mainstream church people should undertake. It is time that churches through national pronouncements and through work by every minister and every lay leader give credence to this idea. It is urgent that they undertake this important work because it is tied to everything the church stands for. The work to ensure a future for generations to come is the single most important issue the leadership of the church can address in this century."

The day will come when nations will be judged not by their military or economic strength, nor by the splendour of their capital cities and public buildings, but by the well-being of their peoples: by their levels of health, nutrition and education; by their opportunities to earn a fair reward for their labours; by their ability to participate in the decisions that affect their lives; by the respect that is shown for their civil and political liberties; by the provision that is made for those who are vulnerable and disadvantaged; and by the protection that is afforded to the growing minds and bodies of their children.

—*The Progress of Nations 1997*
(UNICEF)

Gretchen Eick, of the Office for Church and Society of the United Church of Christ (UCC), encouraged the Council of Bishops to use the authority entrusted to them to institutionalize peace work. It must be made visible and effective at every level of the church. She shared the experience of the UCC in setting up a legislative advocacy network, with 8,000 dedicated coordinators working at every level of the church.

Barbara Thompson, General Secretary of the General Commission on Religion and Race, spoke to the importance of addressing "the concerns of the marginalized who worry about how to survive hour to hour and day by day." She said: "The people who are economically deprived and racial and ethnic minority persons need to be able to take some ownership of this message. You need then to clearly call for peace with justice, not just the absence of war." Addressing the climate of the time, which labeled peacemaking as unpatriotic, she said: "Christians need help in understanding the mandate to confront our government and our structures because we love our country, not because we hate it. They need to understand that because we have such high expectations of our nation and because we really believe that it is possible to make change that we will continue to challenge our nation and help to redirect its energies and its policies."

OUR BIBLICAL MANDATE

All through the Gospels, Jesus challenges the values and practices of a strict patriarchal culture. He reaches out to women with deep compassion, treating them with sensitive concern and honoring their dignity. Often he publicly disobeys cherished norms and laws that oppress women.

Jesus raised from the dead the only son of a widow: "He had compassion for her and said to her, 'Do not weep' " (Luke 7:36-50).

Women were honored members of Jesus' inner circle. The financial resources to sustain his mission were provided by women. Safe houses and meals were offered by women who clearly saw Jesus as the visionary champion of the rights of women. Mary Magdalene, "from whom seven demons had gone out," was a trusted companion. Even a prominent woman of Herod's court, Joanna, wife of Herod's steward, traveled with Jesus and the disciples. Joanna and a number of others "provided for them out of their resources." (Luke 8:1-3).

Touching stories of Mary and Martha and their home, "the house of the poor," in Bethany enrich our understanding of Jesus' compassionate revolt against patriarchy. Mary "sat at the Lord's feet and listened to what he was saying." When Martha complained, Jesus quietly responded, "Mary has chosen the better part, which shall not be taken away from her" (Luke 10:42). It is easy for us to overlook the revolutionary impact of this gracious act. In traditional Jewish law, women were strictly forbidden to study or debate the Torah. This was an act of civil disobedience!

Lest the authorities overlook Jesus' intentions, his disregard for sacred norms and strict laws of patriarchy are enacted in the event of the woman at the well. First, she was a woman, and Jewish men did not carry on conversations with strange women in public. Second, she was a Samaritan woman. Jews would not speak to Samaritans. In fact, they would cross the road to avoid even the hint of social contact. If a Samaritan's shadow fell across the path of a devout Jew, he was obligated to take a difficult journey to the Temple in Jerusalem for cleansing. Third, she was a woman of ill repute. She was an outcast even from the women of her village, as evidenced by her coming to the well at noon. The other women would come in the cool of the evening to talk, laugh, and gossip out of earshot of the men.

Jesus asked for a drink of water. Her sarcastic response came as a rebuke: "How is it that you, a Jew [and, incidentally, a man], ask a drink of me, a woman of Samaria?" (John 4:9). Jesus replied, "If you knew the gift of God, and who it is that is saying to you,

'Give me a drink,' you would have asked him, and he would have given you living water" (John 4:10). Soon she realized that she was being liberated by the messianic presence. The miracle of a transformed life of forgiveness, redemption, and a new sense of dignity and lovability overwhelmed her. She ran to the village in great joy.

The apostle Paul, though a child of patriarchy, caught the vision of Jesus. Again and again in his letters he paid tribute to the women who provided space for the house churches he was organizing across the region. He encouraged many women who were clearly called to apostolic ministry. Hear his words:

> There is no longer Jew or Greek, there is no longer slave or free, there is no longer male and female; for all of you are one in Christ Jesus. And if you belong to Christ, then you are Abraham's offspring, heirs according to the promise. (Gal. 3:28-29)

The apostle offered concrete council in a culture of widespread violence and lawlessness. Notice his advice on how to stop violence at its earliest appearance, in verbal abuse and betrayal of trust:

> So then, putting away falsehood, let all of us speak the truth to our neighbors, for we are members of one another. Be angry but do not sin; do not let the sun go down on your anger, and do not make room for the devil. Thieves must give up stealing; rather let them labor and work honestly with their own hands, so as to have something to share with the needy. Let no evil talk come out of your mouths, but only what is useful for building up, as there is need, so that your words may give grace to those who hear. And do not grieve the Holy Spirit of God, with which you were marked with a seal for the day of redemption. Put away from you all bitterness and wrath and anger and wrangling and slander, together with all malice, and be kind to one another, tender-hearted, forgiving one another as God in Christ has forgiven you. (Eph. 4:25-32)

NOTES

1. Portions of this chapter first appeared in *Teaching Human Sexuality*, ed. Cecile Adams Bean (Nashville: General Board of Discipleship Publications, 1989).

2. Janice Love, "Peacemaking: Commentary on the United Methodist Council of Bishop's Foundation Document In Defense of Creation," unpublished paper, 1988.

3. Ibid.

4. Betty Reardon, *Sexism and the War System*, p. 7. (Teacher's College Press, 1985)

5. Ibid.

6. Kenneth Druck, *The Secrets Men Keep*, p. 13. (New York: Doubleday, 1985).

7. Marc Feigen Fasteau, *The Male Machine* (Delta Books, 1987), p. 189.

8. Reardon, *Sexism and the War System*, p. 48.

9. Alan Geyer, *The Idea of Disarmament* (Elgin, Ill.: Brethren Press, 1996).

10. Susan Perz, ed., *Journal of Sacred Feminine Wisdom* (Claremont, Calif.: Passion Flower Creation, Inc., 1996), p. 48.

Study Guide

Questions for Reflection

How would you define *patriarchy* as described in the text?

How would you describe the relationship between patriarchy and war-making systems?

Does patriarchy play a role in economic injustice?

How is environmental degradation related to patriarchy?

What is the impact of abstract thought on the "masculinization of technology"?

How would you defend your opinion on the role of women in military combat?

What are the unique contributions of women in the building of a just peace?

Suggestions for Local Church Study/Action.

◆ Organize a study/action project on violence in the culture, using the text *A Call to Hope: Living as Christians in a Violent Society.*

◆ Use the Parenting for Peace and Justice and Creating Circles of Peace materials in family night and parenting programs.

◆ With the emerging awareness of the relationship between breast cancer and dioxin in the environment, consider joining the Citizens' Clearing House on Hazardous Waste. Write to them at P.O. Box 6806, Falls Church, VA 22047 (703-237-2249; fax: 703-237-8389).

◆ Join a coalition in your community to provide shelters for victims of domestic violence.

◆ Investigate whether retraining programs are available in your community for men who are addicted to violence.

◆ Sensitize church school workers to the hidden dynamics in classrooms and youth programs that thoughtlessly perpetuate patriarchal assumptions and behavior.

◆ Create opportunities for children and youth to interact with wholesome male role models, as well as female role models: male team-teachers in church school classes for all ages, surrogate parent programs, Big Brothers, Big Sisters, Scouting, etc. Get acquainted with the the Girl Scouts' program Violence Prevention Through Education and Service, designed to teach girls methods of violence prevention.

◆ Write to the World Council of Churches for study materials on the Ecumenical Decade—Churches in Solidarity with Women. Write to WCC Publications, 150 Route de Ferney, 1211 Geneva 2, Switzerland.

◆ If the use of inclusive language in worship is resisted in your congregation, try to involve the pastor and key lay leaders in a study, using some of the current writings of feminist theologians.

◆ Find ways to involve your congregation in the Council of Bishops' Initiative on Children and Poverty, using plans and materials developed by your Annual Conference. Join with child advocacy coalitions to influence public policy affecting children.

◆ Study the biblical texts listed in the "Our Scriptural Mandate" section, using *The Women's Bible Commentary.*

Selected Resources

Studies

A Call to Hope: Living as Christians in a Violent Society, Vera White—this 1997 School of Missions study offers an excellent analysis of the roots of domestic violence. It comes with a built-in study guide, which includes suggestions for activities and action. Order from Friendship Press, P.O. Box 37844, Cincinnati, OH 45222-0844 (513-948-8733).

Creating Circles of Peace, James McGinnis and Kathleen McGinnis—prepared to help families to discover alternatives to violence, this is an excellent kit of tools for educating, motivating, and empowering Christian communities to act against violence. Order from Families Against Violence Advocacy Network, 4144 Lindell Blvd., #408. St. Louis, MO 63108 314-533-4445.

When We All Strong Together, Jennifer Butler and Melissa Gillis—the Presbyterian Church has created a superb study on understanding gender discrimination and building gender justice. A study in seven sessions, themes include, "The Fourth World Conference on Women," "Women's Rights Are Human Rights," "Violence Against Women," "Women and the Media," "Women's Health," and "Girls, Women and Economics." Available from Presbyterian Peacemaking Program, 100 Witherspoon Street, Louisville, KY 40202-1396.

Books

Stopping Rape: A Challenge for Men, Rus Ervin Funk (Philadelphia: New Society Publishers, 1993)—describes and confronts the cultural attitudes that support sexual violence and helps men to understand the impact of rape and sexual assault.

Tough Talk: Men Confronting Men Who Abuse, Joe H. Leonard (Louisville: Presbyterian Publishing House, 1992)—a helpful resource for organizing programs to bring men together to confront domestic violence and abusive language and behavior.

Sex, Violence, and Power in Sports: Rethinking Masculinity, Michael A. Messner and Donald F. Sabo (Freedom, Calif.: The Crossing Press, 1994)—a series of essays exploring the relationship between behavior and attitudes encouraged among male athletes, and violence and sexual assault in the culture of the U.S.

Parenting for Peace and Justice: Ten Years Later, James McGinnis and Kathleen McGinnis (Maryknoll, N.Y., Orbis Books, 1991)—written by and for parents, this book translates the authors' deep social concern into concrete acts of loving, relating, and acting within the family circle. For additional resources, contact the Institute for Peace and Justice, 4144 Lindell Blvd., Rte. 408, St. Louis, MO 63108 (314-533-4445).

Journal of Sacred Feminine Wisdom, issue 1: *Women, Peacemaking, and Surviving War/Global Militarization*, ed. Susan Perz—for a subscription, write to *The Journal of Sacred Feminine Wisdom*, P.O. Box 9, Claremont, CA 91711 (909-626-2333).

UNICEF: State of the World's Children—each year UNICEF publishes the results of global research on trends affecting the children of the world, highlighting emerging issues and suggesting solutions. Order from UNICEF, 3 UN Plaza, New York, NY 10017 (212-326-7000).

Women and War, Jean Vickers (London: Zed Books, 1993)—a good introduction to the main issues surrounding the issue of women and war, raising important questions of human rights and women's rights.

Women Prints: A Detailed Plan of Action for the New Millenium, Ann Smith et al. (Harrisburg: Morehouse Publishing, 1997)—a collection of stories and reflections on the condition of women in the world community, drawing on the momentum in the world's largest gathering of women in history, the UN Fourth World Conference in Beijing in 1995. It was written for Women in Mission and Ministry of the National Episcopal Church.

Speaking Out in the Public Space, Peggy Billings (New York: The Mission Education and Cultivation Program Department for the Women's Division, The United Methodist Church, 1995)—an account of the Section of Christian Social Relations of the Women's Division, 1968–1984. It details the remarkable social witness of women organized for mission in The United Methodist Church over a period of sixteen years. It speaks to the centrality of Christian action in the public sphere and of basic human rights for all in an interdependent world.

Look at the World Through Women's Eyes, ed. Eva Friedlander—this compilation of speeches presented at the NGO Forum on Women 1995 in Beijing reflects the commitment of women to be vital agents in the search for a just, peaceful, and sustainable future. Renowned activists, grassroots organizers, academics, and re-searchers from all over the world analyze the problems faced and solutions offered for the women of the planet. Order from Women, Ink., 777 UN Plaza, New York, NY 10017 (212-687-8633; fax: 212-661-2701).

The Human Rights Watch Global Report on Women's Human Rights (New York: Human Rights Watch, 1995)—women are murdered, beaten, raped, traded as chattel, and denied independence around the world, often with consent of government officials. Today women's groups are organizing to challenge gender-related abuse, collabo-rating with human rights organizations. Human Rights Watch, 485 Fifth Ave., New York, NY 10017-6104.

Freedom from Violence: Women's Strategies from Around the World, ed. Margaret Schuler (New York: UN Development Fund for Women, 1992)—the stories of women are told, as they organize to combat gender violence in twelve nations around the world. Sources of inspiration and common threads of agreement on solutions to gender violence fill these pages. Order from UNIFEM, Widbooks, P.O. Box 20109, Dag Hammarskjöld Convenience Center, New York, NY 10017.

The Progress of Nations 1997 (The United Nations Children Fund [UNICEF])—this annual publication by the UNICEF ranks the nations of the world according to their achievements in child health, nutrition, education, water and sanitation, and progress for women.

APPENDIX

The Universal Declaration of Human Rights

PREAMBLE

Whereas recognition of the inherent dignity and of the equal and inalienable rights of all members of the human family is the foundation of freedom, justice and peace in the world,

Whereas disregard and contempt for human rights have resulted in barbarous acts which have outraged the conscience of mankind, and the advent of a world in which human beings shall enjoy freedom of speech and belief and freedom from fear and want has been proclaimed as the highest aspiration of the common people,

Whereas it is essential, if man is not to be compelled to have recourse, as a last resort, to rebellion against tyrannt and oppression, that human rights should be protected by the rule of law,

Whereas it is essential to promote the development of friendly relations between nations,

Whereas the peoples of the United Nations have in the Charter reaffirmed their faith in fundamental human rights, in the dignity and worth of the human person and in the equal rights of men and women and have determined to promote social progress and better standards of life in larger freedom,

Whereas Member States have pledged themselves to achieve, in co-operation with the United Nations, the promotion of universal respect for and observance of human rights and fundamental freedoms,

Whereas a common understanding of these rights and freedoms is of the greatest importance for the full realization of this pledge,

Now, therefore,

THE GENERAL ASSEMBLY

proclaims

THIS UNIVERSAL DECLARATION OF HUMAN RIGHTS as a common standard of achievement for all peoples and all nations, to the end that every individual and every organ of society, keeping this Declaration constantly in mind, shall strive by teaching and education to promote respect for these rights and freedoms and by progressive measures, national and international, to secure their universal and effective recognition and observance, both among the peoples of Member States themselves and among the peoples of territories under their jurisdiction.

Article 1.

All human beings are born free and equal in dignity and rights. They are endowed with reason and conscience and should act towards one another in a spirit of brotherhood.

Article 2.

Everyone is entitled to all the rights and freedoms set forth in this Declaration, without distinction of any kind, such as race, colour, sex, language, religion, political or other opinion, national or social origin, property, birth or other status. Furthermore, no distinction shall be made on the basis of the political, jurisdictional or international status of the country or territory to which a person belongs, whether it be independent, trust, non-self-governing or under any other limitation of sovereignty.

Article 3.

Everyone has the right to life, liberty and security of person.

Article 4.

No one shall be held in slavery or servitude; slavery and the slave trade shall be prohibited in all their forms.

Article 5.

No one shall be subjected to turture or to cruel, inhuman or degrading treatment or punishment.

Article 6.

Everyone has the right to recognition everywhere as a person before the law.

Article 7.

All are equal before the law and are entitled without any discrimination to equal protection of the law. All are entitled to equal protection against any discrimination in violation of this Declaration and against any incitement to such discrimination.

Article 8.

Everyone has the right to an effective remedy by the competent national tribunals for acts violating the fundamental rights granted him by the constitution or by law.

Article 9.

No one shall be subjected to arbitrary arrest, detention or exile.

Article 10.

Everyone is entitled in full equality to a fair and public hearing by an independent and impartial tribunal, in the determination of his rights and obligations and of any criminal charge against him.

Article 11.

(1) Everyone charged with a penal offence has the right to be presumed innocent until proved guilty according to law in a public trial at which he has had all the guarantees necessary for his defence.

(2) No one shall be held guilty of any penal offence on account of any act or omission which did not constitute a penal offence, under national or international law, at the time when it was committed. Nor shall a heavier penalty be imposed than the one that was applicable at the time the penal offence was committed.

Article 12.

No one shall be subjected to arbitrary interference with his privacy, family, home or correspondence, nor to attacks upon his honour and reputation. Everyone has the right to the protection of the law against such interference or attacks.

Article 13.

(1) Everyone has the right to freedom of movement and residence within the borders of each state.

(2) Everyone has the right to leave any country, including his own, and to return to his country.

Article 14.

(1) Everyone has the right to seek and to enjoy in other countries asylum from persecution.

(2) This right may not be invoked in the case of prosecutions genuinely arising from non-political crimes or from acts contrary to the purposes and principles of the United Nations.

Article 15.

(1) Everyone has the right to a nationality.

(2) No one shall be arbitrarily deprived of his nationality nor denied the right to change his nationality.

Article 16.
(1) Men and women of full age, without any limitation due to race, nationality or religion, have the right to marry and to found a family. They are entitled to equal rights as to marriage, during marriage and at its dissolution.
(2) Marriage shall be entered into only with the free and full consent of the intending spouses.
(3) The family is the natural and fundamental group unit of society and is entitled to protection by society and the State.

Article 17.
(1) Everyone has the right to own property alone as well as in association with others.
(2) No one shall be arbitrarily deprived of his property.

Article 18.
Everyone has the right to freedom of thought, conscience and religion; this right includes freedom to change his religion or belief, and freedom, either alone or in community with others and in public or private, to manifest his religion or belief in teaching, practice, worship and observance.

Article 19.
Everyone has the right to freedom of opinion and expression; this right includes freedom to hold opinions without interference and to seek, receive and impart information and ideas through any media and regardless of frontiers.

Article 20.
(1) Everyone has the right to freedom of peaceful assembly and association.
(2) No one may be compelled to belong to an association.

Article 21.
(1) Everyone has the right to take part in the government of his country, directly or through freely chosen representatives.
(2) Everyone has the right of equal access to public service in his country.
(3) The will of the people shall be the basis of the authority of government; this will shall be express in periodic and genuine elections which shall be by universal and equal suffrage and shall be held by secret vote or by equivalent free voting procedures.

Article 22.
Everyone, as a member of society, has the right to social security and is entitled to realization, through national effort and international co-operation and in accordance with the organization and resources of each State, of the economic, social and cultural rights indispensable for his dignity and the free development of his personality.

Article 23.
(1) Everyone has the right to work, to free choice of employment, to just and favourable conditions of work and to protection against unemployment.
(2) Everyone, without any discrimination, has the right to equal pay for equal work.
(3) Everyone who works has the right to just and favourable remuneration ensuring for himself and his family an existence worthy of human dignity, and supplemented, if necessary, by other means of social protection.
(4) Everyone has the right to form and to join trade unions for the protection of his interests.

Article 24.
Everyone has the right to rest and leisure, including reasonable limitation of working hours and periodic holidays with pay.

Article 25.
(1) Everyone has the right to a standard of living adequate for the health and well-being of himself and of his family, including food, clothing, housing and medical care and necessary social services, and the right to security in the event of unemployment, sickness, disability, widowhood, old age or other lack of livelihood in circumstances beyond his control.
(2) Motherhood and childhood are entitled to special care and assistance. All children, whether born in or out of wedlock, shall enjoy the same social protection.

Article 26.
(1) Everyone has the right to education. Education shall be free, at least in the elementary and fundamental stages. Elementary education shall be compulsory. Technical and professional education shall be made generally available and higher education shall be equally accessible to all on the basis of meric.
(2) Education shall be directed to the full development of the human personality and to the strengthening of respect for human rights and fundamental freedoms. It shall promote understanding, tolerance and friendship among all nations, racial or religious groups, and shall further the activities of the United Nations for the maintenance of peace.
(3) Parents have a prior right to choose the kind of education that shall be given to their children.

Article 27.
(1) Everyone has the right freely to participate in the cultural life of the community, to enjoy the arts and to share in scientific advancement and its benefits.
(2) Everyone has the right to the protection of the moral and material interests resulting from any scientific, literary or artistic production of which he is the author.

Article 28.
Everyone is entitled to a social and international order in which the rights and freedoms set forth in this Declaration can be fully realized.

Article 29.
(1) Everyone has duties to the community in which alone the free and full development of his personality is possible.
(2) In the exercise of his rights and freedoms, everyone shall be subject only to such limitations as are determined by law solely for the purpose of securing due recognition and respect for the rights and freedoms of others and of meeting the just requirements of morality, public order and the general welfare in a democratic society.
(3) These rights and freedoms may in no case be exercised contrary to the purposes and principles of the United Nations.

Article 30.
Nothing in this Declaration may be interpreted as implying for any State, group or person any right to engage in any activity or to perform any act aimed at the destruction of any of the rights and freedoms set forth herein.

"RESOLUTION ON OBSERVANCE OF THE FIFTIETH ANNIVERSARY OF *THE UNIVERSAL DECLARATION OF HUMAN RIGHTS*"

(Adopted by the General Assembly of the NCCC USA on November 13, 1997).

WHEREAS: December 10, 1998 will mark the 50th anniversary of the Universal Declaration of Human Rights by the United Nations; and

WHEREAS: the Universal Declaration of Human Rights and the International Covenants on Economic, Social, and Cultural Rights and Civil and Political Rights serve as the universally accepted standards of human rights and as such provide an outstanding achievement worthy of recognition and celebration; and

WHEREAS: we are daily reminded that individuals and communities suffer often because essential human freedoms are not recognized, just treatment and protections are not guaranteed, and violations of the wholeness and integrity of personhood are not prevented throughout the world, including the United States; and

WHEREAS: the United States of America, with its potential for creative human rights leadership, has yet to ratify major international human rights instruments; and

WHEREAS: our religious faith calls us to affirm the dignity and worth of every human being and to struggle for justice for oppressed people everywhere, and

WHEREAS: the General Assembly of the United Nations, reflecting the gross violations of human rights during World War II, also in 1948 unanimously adopted the Genocide Convention, calling for the protection of "national, ethnic, racial and religious" groups from activities that would harm or destroy them; and calling for competent international judicial mechanisms with jurisdiction over such crimes;

THEREFORE: the General Assembly of the National Council of Churches of Christ in the United States of America, meeting in Washington, DC, November 13, 1997:

CALLS upon the units of the Council and its member communions to observe and celebrate 1998 as Universal Human Rights Year, an occasion to strengthen our commitment to the advancement of human rights through widespread dissemination, study and reflection of the Universal Declaration and other international human rights instruments in order to promote tolerance, understanding and greater respect for human rights,

URGES the United States Congress, the President and the Administration to reaffirm United States commitment to universal human rights, and to work toward the ratification and implementation of international human rights instruments, including the International Covenant on Economic, Social and Cultural Rights, the Convention on the Elimination of all Forms of Discrimination Against Women, and the Convention on the Rights of the Child;

CALLS urgent attention to contemporary threats to national, ethnic, racial and religious groups, through the revival of ancient hatreds, and the fostering of fear, with the potential for genocidal consequences, and further calls for the strengthening of the international judicial system to include an international criminal court with jurisdiction over individuals responsible for gross violations of human rights, such as, genocidal and war crimes and other crimes against humanity.

"A CALL TO ACTION"

This week at the First National People of Color Environmental Leadership Summit in Washington, DC, a new international movement of indigenous and grassroots peoples was born. It is a multi-racial, multi-cultural convergence of existing local and regional grassroots movements and struggles which are already underway by people of color which are actively resisting various forms of environmental genocide against them throughout the world. We have come from all states of the U.S., Central and South America, the Caribbean, Hawaii, Puerto Rico, Alaska, Marshall Islands and Canada.

We are a new movement which raises the life and death struggles of indigenous and grassroots communities of color to an unprecedented multi-national integrated level. The fight against the disproportionately harmful impact of environmental degradation upon peoples of color is not new. We have always been in this struggle; we have always known what is at stake. This movement addresses every aspect of our quality of life. Unlike traditional mainstream environmental and social justice organizations, this multi-racial, multi-cultural movement of peoples of color is evolving from the bottom up and not the top down. It seeks a global vision based on grassroots realities.

We call for an immediate end to the systematic murder of peoples of color through Global environmental genocide.

We refuse to accept the deliberate targeting of communities of color and the lands of indigenous peoples as dumping grounds for hazardous wastes and radioactive materials, and the production of pollutants.

We call on the president of the U.S., the congress, and all federal, state, and local agencies to discontinue all policies and practices of environmental racism and to properly enforce existing environmental protection laws and policies.

We call for a ban on the export of hazardous waste and radioactive materials that are devastating the world, particularly the lands of peoples of color.

We demand full reparations for all past injustices and further demand an immediate halt to all schemes that degrade the lives and lands of peoples of color with harmful development and hazardous waste disposal.

We call for a restructuring of the traditional relationships of mainstream environmental organizations and activists of communities of color and grassroots and indigenous peoples.

We demand the right to live in drug free, healthy communities, free of the illnesses and disease spawned by environmental degradation which affects our children, youth and families.

We call for the embodiment of our ratified Principles of Environmental Justice in grassroots social and political work within communities of color.

We call for an end to war, violence and militarism, because these are among the most environmentally and ecologically destructive phenomena known to humankind, and millions of people of color have perished due to war.

We are here; We are united; We are strong; We are one! We have come together speaking out of our cultural diversity to our common oppression, as many members of one family—Asians and Asian Americans, Pacific Islanders and Pacific Americans, Native Peoples and Alaskans, Latinos and Canadians, Latin Americans and Central Americans, Africans and African Americans. In our collective unity, there is great strength. We have come together around many issues in many lands to unleash the power of our united will in a common struggle for a new environmental movement—a movement to eradicate environmental racism and bring into being true social justice and self-determination.

As peoples of color, we have not chosen our struggles; they have chosen us. We suffer disproportionate victimization by environmental degradation and a host of other forms of social economic and political violence. We have no choice but to come together to overcome our common barriers and resist our common foes. Only in the diversity of our oppression are we able to clearly see the pervasive pattern of genocidal environmental racism. We gathered to speak for ourselves and to define the issues in our own way.

For more information contact J.D. Hanson at the General Board of Church and Society of The United Methodist Church, 100 Maryland Ave., NE, Washington, D.C., 20002 (202-488-5600).